Marketing to
Millennials

Marketing to
Millennials

● ●

Reach the Largest and
Most Influential Generation
of Consumers Ever

JEFF FROMM and CHRISTIE GARTON

AMERICAN MANAGEMENT ASSOCIATION

New York • Atlanta • Brussels • Chicago • Mexico City • San Francisco
Shanghai • Tokyo • Toronto • Washington, D.C.

Bulk discounts available. For details visit:
www.amacombooks.org/go/specialsales
Or contact special sales:
Phone: 800-250-5308
E-mail: specialsls@amanet.org
View all the AMACOM titles at: www.amacombooks.org
American Management Association: www.amanet.org

This publication is designed to provide accurate and authoritative information in regard to the subject matter covered. It is sold with the understanding that the publisher is not engaged in rendering legal, accounting, or other professional service. If legal advice or other expert assistance is required, the services of a competent professional person should be sought.

Library of Congress Cataloging-in-Publication Data

Fromm, Jeff.
  Marketing to millennials : reach the largest and most influential generation of consumers ever / Jeff Fromm and Christie Garton.
      pages cm
  Includes bibliographical references and index.
  ISBN 978-0-8144-3322-5 (hardcover)—ISBN 0-8144-3322-7 (hardcover)
  1. Young adult consumers—Attitudes.   2. Generation Y—Attitudes.   3. Target marketing.   4. Consumer behavior.   I. Garton, Christie.   II. Title.
  HF5415.332.Y66F76 2013
  658.8'340842—dc23
                                    2013007818

About AMA
American Management Association (www.amanet.org) is a world leader in talent development, advancing the skills of individuals to drive business success. Our mission is to support the goals of individuals and organizations through a complete range of products and services, including classroom and virtual seminars, webcasts, webinars, podcasts, conferences, corporate and government solutions, business books, and research. AMA's approach to improving performance combines experiential learning—learning through doing—with opportunities for ongoing professional growth at every step of one's career journey.

Printing number
10 9 8 7 6 5 4 3 2 1

To the Millennials: We can't wait to see what you come up with next!

Contents

Figures

Foreword

It feels like yesterday when my husband and I bought our oldest daughter her own personal computer. One night, my husband and I wondered why it was so quiet in the house. We thought the three kids—our oldest daughter and our twins—were upstairs in their rooms, sleeping or doing homework. When I went upstairs to check, I found them sitting on my oldest daughter's bed hunting and pecking on the computer with the television on and the radio playing. They were completely enthralled with the new technology in front of them, while simultaneously listening to music and watching TV. This capability to multitask with various kinds of technology immediately stood out to me. With a constant connection to the outside world, I knew my children's generation would inevitably be part of the most influential generation of workers and consumers ever.

Today, my oldest daughter is 25 and the twins are 17. They fit perfectly in the Millennial cohort. I converse with them as consumers and listen closely to their opinions to ensure I maintain a fresh perspective. As the chief marketer for Applebee's, our brand's future depends on being relevant and attracting this very large group of tech-savvy, highly independent, and creative thinkers. Understanding what motivates them, what drives them, and how they consume media is all-important work.

This is where Jeff Fromm and Christie Garton's new book, *Marketing to Millennials*, comes in.

Millennials are different. Boomers grew up answering the question "Where were you when President John F. Kennedy was shot?" Millennials answer the question of where they were on the day of the 9/11 attack. Boomers grew up with racial tension and cultural divides, and Millennials helped elect the first African-American president. Boomers went to the library; Millennials access Google. Boomers signed yearbooks; Millennials log in to Facebook.

Though Millennial attitudes and behaviors can be unfamiliar and challenging, this book facilitates an understanding and appreciation of this generation.

Christie is a Millennial herself, and Millennials are a topic close to Jeff's heart. He has three children, two of whom, at 21, are Millennial twins. In addition to coauthoring articles and regularly speaking about Millennials at various events, Jeff also coauthored a report called "American Millennials: Deciphering the Enigma Generation," based on a joint study conducted by Barkley, The Boston Consulting Group (BCG), and Service Management Group. The findings from this research are the foundation for this book. They yielded insights that provide practical frameworks for building business strategy, product ideas, and marketing and media plans, as well as for better aligning corporate cultures with Millennial values.

Marketing to Millennials is a must-read for all of us who hire, coach, and market with Millennials. Notice I said market *with* Millennials, as it is no longer acceptable to market *to* your target audience. Today, we converse and connect with Millennials to build their trust and earn loyalty. We once commanded and provided feedback. We now coach and provide feed forward.

Jeff and Christie explain that this group of 84 million young adults does things dramatically differently from generations prior. They prefer texting to talking. They join companies for their values not just their cultures. They graduate from high school, go to college, get married, and have children, but not necessarily in that order.

Walk up and down the halls of your offices and many of them are wearing headphones and listening to music. While that made me a little crazy at first, that's how they get things done. Send out an e-mail in the middle of the night and they respond. Trying to keep them off their cell phones is impossible. They like cocreating products and services, and, if they participate in the cocreation process, Millennials are more likely to share and endorse. They are adventurous eaters and more likely to try new foods and flavors. They are skilled and they are educated, and they have been told they can do anything.

So here we have it, a whole new workforce and a whole new generation of consumers. Dive into this book and learn about the unique Millennials. This book will give you new insights and strategic tools that will enable you to reach out and connect with this enormous crowd of free-spirited and optimistic young adults called the Millennial generation.

—Becky Johnson
Chief Marketer,
Applebee's

Acknowledgments

From Both of Us

A big thanks must go to the Millennial thought leaders, brand leaders, and experts and entrepreneurs who graciously gave their time and insights throughout the writing of this book. Thanks also to Ellen Kadin and Erika Spelman at AMACOM, and to Ginny Carroll at North Market Street Graphics, for patiently guiding us through the publication process. Without our agent, Loretta Barrett, we would not have had the good fortune of working with them.

From Jeff Fromm

In the marketing world, we are always looking for the sweet spot—fresh and actionable insights. It's a search that we at Barkley engage in daily for our clients, but it was our colleague Brad Hanna who suggested we chronicle our knowledge about American Millennial consumers. For that encouragement, thank you, Brad.

Any successful venture requires resources, equipment, and skill (plus a little luck). Without the full backing of Barkley's CEO, Jeff King, who encouraged us to plunge ahead, this book wouldn't have left the ground. Many other colleagues also played key roles, and we'd specifically like to express our gratitude to Mark Logan, Joe Cox, Kim Boyer, Jason Parks, Joe Sciara, and Geoff Pickering for their feedback. To Aziz Giga for his thoughtful comments on the manuscript, thank you.

In early 2011, when we started planning the book, it was obvious that the Millennial generation was having an enormous financial impact on the economy and workforce, one that would only increase. What wasn't obvious, though, was how to tap into that influence. We wanted to better understand the sociological, technological, and behavioral underpinnings of Millennials' consumer habits.

Toward that end, we invited Christine Barton of The Boston Consulting Group (BCG) and Chris Egan of Service Management Group (SMG) to embark on a comprehensive research study of American Millennials. Fortunately for us, they agreed. They and their teams brought expertise and professionalism. Most important, they analyzed reams of survey results and uncovered fascinating insights. This book draws heavily on our joint research, as well as BCG's segmentation analysis, and we are grateful to Cheryl Uynicky, Sean Bramble, David Rowlee, Joe Cardador, and all the others from BCG and SMG who contributed.

This book evolved from our initial report, "American Millennials: Deciphering the Enigma Generation." Barkley partner and social media whiz Celeste Lindell deserves massive credit for taking the research findings and writing an engaging narrative about what makes Millennials tick.

After our research was finished, we wanted to share it with marketing and strategy professionals, but we didn't just want to push it out. We wanted a conversation, a community. Hence, the idea for a full-blown conference on marketing to Millennials came to us, and we dubbed it Share.Like.Buy (www.sharelikebuy.com). We are indebted to Nathan James, who partnered with us on the first, second, and now third annual conferences.

We could not have gotten this book to publication without our talented and persistent support team: Lainie Decker, who has helped with almost every aspect of the research, report, articles, presentations, conferences, and book, and Andrea Franz, whose cheerfulness and attention to detail kept us organized, coordinated, and on schedule.

My wife, Rhonda Fromm, intimately understands the difference between generational attributes and life stages because we have, after 24 years, been through most of them together. During the consuming process of writing this book, she has kept our lives on course, and I'm deeply grateful. Truth be told, my deepest gratitude goes to my three children, Scott (16), Abby (21), and Laura (21), who motivated me to immerse myself in understanding the Millennial mindset, if for no other reason than to appear hip. And, of course, to my parents, Bill and Bernie, and my brothers, Andy and Dan, thank you. You are the best parents and brothers anyone could have asked for and I thank you for your unyielding support.

From Christie Garton

This book is the product of a lot of hard work, support, and passion from an incredible group of talented people—many of them already mentioned. I want to also thank my parents, Jim and Nancy, and my grandfather Bill for their endless support. You have always been there for me, supporting my entrepreneurial endeavors from the very beginning. Thanks also to my adventure-loving husband and soul mate, Matt. You keep me inspired.

Marketing to
Millennials

Introduction

Get ready, America. With more than 80 million in their ranks, the Millennials (born between 1977 and 1995) are taking center stage. Comprising roughly 25 percent of the U.S. population, as a group they are larger than the Baby Boomers (born 1946 to 1964) and three times the size of Generation X (born 1965 to 1976).

But it's not just their size that's impressive. Collectively, they are exerting their power and influence like no generation that's come before.

In the United States, Millennials are flexing their political muscle, having been widely credited with helping to elect the country's first African-American president.

Look to the business world, and you'll find entrepreneurial-minded Millennials launching multi-*billion*-dollar companies from the comfort of their college dorm rooms.

Hispanics are the largest ethnic minority among Millennials, followed by African-Americans. Indeed, Millennials are more ethnically diverse than previous generations.

Given their size, diversity, and influence on culture and brands, it's no surprise that the world has taken note. While many stories and studies over the past decade from organizations such as Lifecourse Associates and Pew Research Center addressed their social and media consumption habits, their entry into the workplace, and, yes, their proclivity for technology, little has been documented about Millennials *as active consumers.*

Until now.

Influential and Active Consumers

Businesses cannot afford to ignore the Millennials. Their collective buying power alone—an estimated $200 billion annually—is *already* noteworthy and will only increase as they mature into their peak earning and spending years.

They're a vital part of the market with their *indirect* annual spending power estimated to be $500 billion, largely because of their strong influence on their parents.

To be sure, the recent economic recession has impacted their near-term spending. Nevertheless, this generation, regardless of its current earning power, engages with brands in new and different ways that have tangible implications for a company's bottom line.

But let's face it. It's hard—if not impossible—to market to a generation you don't understand. Unfortunately, there was no resource to which we could point Barkley's clients—outside of one-off articles in business magazines or trade publications—that would provide a clear and big-picture view of this new and important generation of consumers.

Barkley is an independent advertising agency based in Kansas City, Missouri, with a major focus on "What's Next." Based on this focus, Barkley has invested heavily in Millennial consumer trends research.

So, in 2011 and 2012, we set out to learn more about this generation, conducting consumer research with global management consulting firm The Boston Consulting Group (BCG) (www.bcg.com) and international customer research firm Service Management Group (SMG) (www.smg.com) through a robust panel study that would shed light on Millennial consumers and their behavior.

The three firms participated in the design and structure of the survey questions. SMG administered the survey; they obtained the online panel, scrubbed the responses for data validity, and generated the statistical output. Analysis of the survey results was a joint effort among all partners. The online random panel sample was composed of 4,259 Millennials (eligible ages 16 to 34) and 1,234 non-Millennials (eligible ages 35 to 74).

With 5,493 survey respondents and more than 4 million data points, a detailed analytical plan was developed to mine the survey results for key trends and specific insights. All respondents (n = 5,493) answered questions regarding lifestyle (health and wellness), social and political issues, cause marketing, and digital, social, and mobile usage.

Based on screening questions, respondents then qualified for one of four additional question sets regarding preferences and habits related to Grocery (Consumer Packaged Goods), Travel, Restaurant, and Apparel (Retail). Markets were segmented by:

- General cohort
- Gender
- Frequency and spend
- Household income
- Household composition
- Race/ethnicity (Hispanic, non-Hispanic)

In September 2011, Barkley published a report called "American Millennials: Deciphering the Enigma Generation" based on this research.

Fast-forward to today: With 4,000+ Millennial and 1,000+ older-generation survey responses, extensive consumer interviews, and hours of analysis behind us, this book reveals our findings.

What We Uncovered

When our study first began to take shape, we spent a long time looking at earlier findings. Most—if not all—publications tended to view Millennials as a homogeneous group.

Not only did our joint research unequivocally prove this wrong, but BCG went one step further by developing a segmentation model that divides Millennials into six major subgroups.

This information is invaluable to any company that wants to target its marketing efforts more efficiently and effectively to this generation's tastemakers and influencers.

Another key focus of our study was to identify how behaviors and attitudes differ between Millennials and non-Millennials—and to determine which of those differences are truly characteristic of the generation and not simply related to Millennials' youth or their relatively early stage of life.

Beyond their widely recognized affinity for technology, our research identified specific behaviors and attitudes that the Millennials are likely to bring with them into their next life stages. Each of these characteristic attitudes—explained in detail in the first several chapters—has implications for companies, their brands, and the leaders, who will need to adapt to an era of cocreation and two-way communication in which the new consumer clearly has a strong voice.

Our research also found that Millennials are leading indicators (if not the drivers) of media consumption, advocacy, and social media usage among all generations. For instance, Facebook—created by Mark Zuckerberg, one of the most famous Millennials—began as a college-based social network. Today, it has a diverse pool of users with an average age of 38, not 18. The bottom line: Brands, old and new, cannot afford to ignore this generation.

Here's a quick snapshot of what else you can expect to find in this book:

- *Who they are.* You'll hear directly from the influential and characteristic members of this generation, providing an intimate look at Millennial consumers.

- *The New Rules of Marketing to Millennials.* Brands are no longer in control of their own image and message with this generation. Indeed, a key finding from our study was that Millennials derive value from being engaged in product development, advertising, social interactions, and other facets of the marketing process. Because their participation and cocreation are likely to result in completely new marketing disciplines that tie in to Millennials' fast-paced lifestyles, we've laid out the new rules of marketing *with* this generation.

- *Case studies.* From long-established youth brands like MTV to fresh start-up concepts like Dollar Shave Club, we've identified several organizations that are getting it right when it comes to marketing to Millennials.

Ready to cast aside the old rules of marketing *at* these consumers? When it comes to Millennials, the new rules of engagement reign.

Who Are They?

Meet Janelle, age 27.

Stretched across the hood of a Ford Fiesta in a loving embrace, her Facebook photo could easily be an ad for Ford.

Perhaps it is?

Nope. Janelle just happens to love her car. A lot. And the best way she knows how to say it is to show it to all her friends—and their friends (and so forth)—on Facebook.

Simple as that.

Well, actually, it's not so simple. For a company like Ford that wants to remain relevant, understanding Janelle's very public display of affection couldn't be more crucial.

A decade ago, a consumer of Janelle's age might have simply shared her affinity for Ford with her closest group of friends, and maybe one or two would be tempted to take a test drive. But thanks to digital and social tools like Facebook, her photo can now be seen far and wide. Janelle's power to influence others is exponentially higher today than it would have been in the past.

The Participation Economy

Not willing to be passive consumers any longer, this generation wants to actively participate, cocreate, and, most important, be included as partners in the brands they love. Often, the cocreation process begins with the product or service design, includes the customer journey or shopping experience, and is more easily seen in the marketing and social media space closer to the end of the marketing cycle. In fact, one could argue that functional and emotional benefits alone will not be enough for your brand to thrive with this generation since Millennial brand fans feel they have a shared interest in the brand's success.

Welcome to the participation economy.

Former Medtronic CEO and Harvard Business School professor Bill George provided a good summary of the participation economy concept back in 2009, when it was in its more nascent stage: "People are their own medium, their own creation. You have to let them in, [l]et consumers move your ideas along. They want to interact. Measure 'Return on Involvement' not 'Return on Investment.' "[1]

It's a huge shift that youth-focused brands like MTV and Frito-Lay (which you'll hear more about later) were some of the first to notice and address this in their strategy process.

But just a few short years later, the participation economy has arrived at the doorstep of *all* companies, fundamentally impacting not only their marketing tactics but how they do business as well, and we are only just beginning to understand its full implications.

The Old Framework vs. the Participation Framework

In the past, consumers were rarely part of the product development and marketing process. Outside of focus groups done in person or by phone, instantaneous feedback channels like Facebook, Twitter, and crowdsourced ratings and review websites like Yelp didn't exist. (See Figure 1-1.)

Driven by advances in digital and mobile technology, consumers of all ages can participate in these once closed-door processes, and many are accepting, if not demanding, the invitation. For Millennials, it's almost an expectation that companies should want to seek their opinion.

In one successful instance, craft beer brewer Samuel Adams took an unprecedented step by letting Facebook fans create a new brew. To crowdsource ideas, the company used an app called the CrowdCraft Project on Facebook, helping to determine the beer's color, clarity, body, hops, and malt. The ideas that garnered the most votes were incorporated into the beer, which was served

THE PARTICIPATION ECONOMY

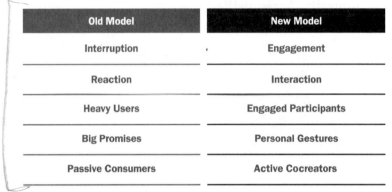

Old Model	New Model
Interruption	Engagement
Reaction	Interaction
Heavy Users	Engaged Participants
Big Promises	Personal Gestures
Passive Consumers	Active Cocreators

Source: Barkley, The Boston Consulting Group, and Service Management Group, "American Millennials: Deciphering the Enigma Generation," September 2011.

Figure 1-1 An overview of the participation economy.

at the popular South by Southwest Festival in Austin, Texas, and at the Samuel Adams Boston Brewery in Boston, Massachusetts.

For an example from the tech industry, consider how the Android line of cell phones demonstrated that it's good for business to include consumers in the product development process. Android's mobile operating system is the polar opposite of Apple's iOS. Indeed, Android uses an *open-source* network that allows users to improve the system by building add-ons and apps.[2] This endeavor, launched in collaboration with Google, allows for cocreation, innovation, and consumer feedback. The goal is to create a network where everyone can contribute to making the best product possible. Talk about valuing the customer's opinion!

On the other hand, Apple's closed and proprietary approach draws criticism from digital rights advocates such as the Electronic Frontier Foundation (EFF) for creating a "crystal prison" for developers and end users. At issue are restrictions imposed by the design of iOS, namely: "digital rights management (DRM) intended to lock purchased media to Apple's platform, the development model (requiring a yearly subscription to distribute apps developed for the iOS), the centralized approval process for apps, as well as Apple's general control and lockdown of the platform itself," according to Wikipedia.[3]

"This issue doesn't come as much of a surprise to anyone who has become involved with Apple products," Simon Sage, blogger and editor-at-large of Mobile Nations, wrote. "It's hard not to get an iPhone and Mac and not know that from here on in, you're expected to do things The Apple Way."[4]

The end result? An inferior product, says none other than Steve Wozniak, cofounder of Apple, according to the EFF.[5] "[N]o place, and no system, can be perfect if it denies its citizens the freedom to change it, or the freedom to leave," says an EFF report.[6]

It can also impact sales. In late 2011, iOS accounted for 60 percent of the market share for smartphones and tablet computers. However by mid-2012, iOS had slipped to just 16.9 percent and Android had taken over with 68.1 percent global share.[7] While a direct link between Android's open network approach and increasing market share is a bit of a stretch, it is undeniably a contributing factor.

Certainly, we are witnessing an increasing number of brands turning to social media to tap consumer insights and engage fans of all ages, but where we are really seeing the most engagement—the *participation economy* at play—is with Millennials.

So what got us here? Although non-Millennial generations value personal connection, our study found that Millennials use technology to connect with a greater number of people, more frequently, and in real time. Not only are they using social media platforms more than non-Millennials, they maintain significantly larger networks and influence.

Indeed, 46 percent of Millennial survey respondents reported having 200 or more Facebook "friends," compared to 19 percent of non-Millennials, as you can see in Figure 1-2.

MILLENNIALS HAVE MORE FRIENDS

Number of connections on social networks is significantly larger

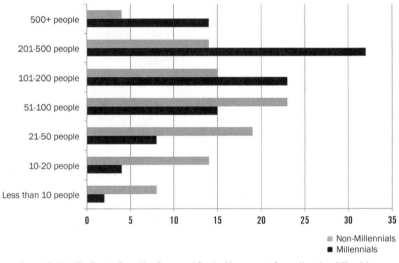

Source: Barkley, The Boston Consulting Group, and Service Management Group, "American Millennials: Deciphering the Enigma Generation," September 2011.

Figure 1-2 Millennials have more online connections.

It's not just about the size of their network. Millennials report that they gain a psychological boost when engaging with their online friends. This is a significant shift between generations. In fact, Millennials reported that they feel they are missing out when they are not up to date on social media chatter, and they feel vali-dated when the community "likes" their posts—especially when they are the first to review a product or service or give advice to a friend on a purchase decision. As shown in Figure 1-3, Millennials overwhelmingly agree (47 percent vs. 28 percent) that their lives feel richer when they're connected to more people through social media connections.

Given these findings, it comes as no surprise that Millennials are also off the chart when it comes to their willingness to give companies feedback. In fact, they find increased brand value and preference when they provide marketing and strategy professionals with their views.

"Millennials are a very open generation, and a great resource for brands, as cocreation is second nature for them," says Jacqueline Anderson, director of product development at J.D. Power and Associates and former Millennial-focused senior analyst at Forrester Research. "If you're facing a challenge as a brand, reach out."

In the apparel industry, social shopping site Krush is another example of a company that is effectively tapping consumer insight. In this case, it's to boost the bottom line. Krush, a Boston-based start-up, addresses the age-old dilemma of retailers losing millions of dollars on products that never sell because they don't have a clue what consumers want. They do this by offering retail brands a platform where they can go directly to their key site users, ages 15 to 30, with "Exclusive SneakPeeks" or previews of upcoming lines in order to gauge how successful they'll be when they hit the stores.

These consumers are encouraged not to hold back on their critiques but, instead, to be vocal about their opinions, setting the trends rather than following them.[8] At the end of a Sneak-Peek, each Krush brand receives an in-depth report that sum-

MILLENNIALS VALUE SOCIAL NETWORKING

Social media connections enrich their lives daily

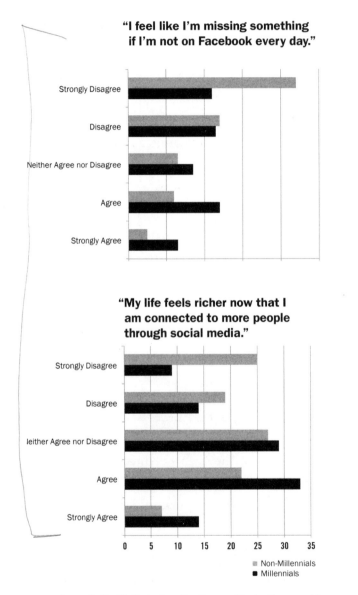

Source: Barkley, The Boston Consulting Group, and Service Management Group, "American Millennials: Deciphering the Enigma Generation," September 2011.

Figure 1-3 Millennials value social media.

marizes all consumer feedback including which demographics prefer which items—and at which locations. Not only is this an effective means of crowdsourcing, but it also helps brands reduce risk by letting them know in advance what to double down on and what should be considered for the chopping block.

Krush is an important example of how predictive analytics, when overlaid with social media to allow for consumer feedback, can be a beneficial tool for predicting future fashion trends. This predictive ability is especially important these days in the fashion world, where more and more consumers take their style cues from the social networks rather than from traditional influencers such as runway shows and fashion magazines. These young consumers want to participate, and, thus, they appreciate the opportunity to have what could possibly end up being a significant impact on their favorite brands' strategic decisions. So it's a win-win, with both parties benefiting.

Because "participation" is now part of the value equation, this opens up a range of exciting possibilities for companies when it comes to engaging the Millennial generation. Indeed, our study found they *want* brands to engage with them through social media. As Figure 1-4 shows, Millennials *expect* brands to participate in social media.

The bottom line? It's no longer about providing the product or service but about giving Millennials a voice and an opportunity to participate in product development and marketing that drives increased brand preference. Companies that act on this insight win big. We'll flesh out the participation economy model more in the coming chapters. But first, let's get back to Janelle and her Ford Fiesta.

MILLENNIALS EXPECT BRANDS TO PARTICIPATE IN SOCIAL MEDIA

They seek out brands in social media and value a social presence

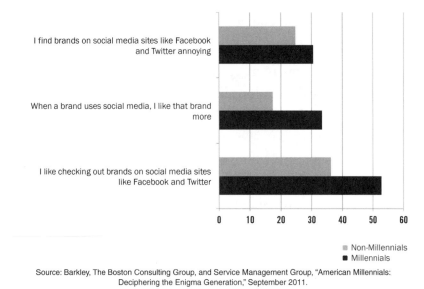

Source: Barkley, The Boston Consulting Group, and Service Management Group, "American Millennials: Deciphering the Enigma Generation," September 2011.

Figure 1-4 Millennials seek brand participation.

Friends Have Influence

When Janelle began her car search, where did she turn for advice? Facebook, of course. Her 2,000+ friends have become a key source of information and support.

"I personally know everyone I'm friends with. They are very loyal and vocal whenever I've needed advice. I value their input," says Janelle. "So when I began my car search, they had a lot of say."

After giving them her criteria—a good-looking, American-made car with great gas mileage at an affordable price—her friends helped her narrow down her choices to three cars, which included the Ford Fiesta.

Janelle wasn't done with her research. She also happens to be active on Twitter, and, although she has only 700 followers, she views this group as an important source of information because its members fall outside of her direct network of contacts.

"I use it more to get an outside opinion, to get a different perspective," she explains.

So she took her top three choices to her followers and asked them to decide the winner. The Ford Fiesta came out on top. After a quick trip with her dad to the local Ford dealer, where she fell in love with the silver one on the lot, Janelle was sold.

Unfortunately, there was a tiny snag in the plan. Janelle wasn't the only one wanting that exact make and model of the Fiesta. According to her car dealer, it was on back order and wouldn't be available for several months. Janelle was dismayed. Having already spent a year hunting for a car, she couldn't wait any longer.

Let's take a break in the story for a quick review. So far, we have gotten a glimpse of how one Millennial is using social media for consumer research and purchasing decisions.

At no point did an advertisement directly influence Janelle's decision. She first wanted input from her friends and contacts. This is a common approach that Millennials take when researching their options, as Jacqueline Anderson explains: "From a Millennial's perspective, you don't make a decision without your friends." Our data back this up, as you can see in Figure 1-5.

But now that a wrench had been thrown into Janelle's plan to purchase a Ford Fiesta, the playing field was wide open. Suddenly, her second favorite choice, the Chevy Sonic, was pulling ahead.

MILLENNIALS ARE HEAVILY INFLUENCED BY THEIR PEERS

Seek peer input and affirmation on decisions

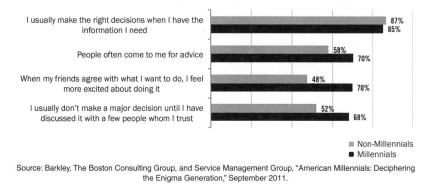

I usually make the right decisions when I have the information I need — 87% / 85%

People often come to me for advice — 58% / 70%

When my friends agree with what I want to do, I feel more excited about doing it — 48% / 70%

I usually don't make a major decision until I have discussed it with a few people whom I trust — 52% / 68%

Non-Millennials
Millennials

Source: Barkley, The Boston Consulting Group, and Service Management Group, "American Millennials: Deciphering the Enigma Generation," September 2011.

Figure 1-5 Millennial value placed on peer affirmation.

Taking to Twitter once again to share her dismay and decision to shift gears, Janelle decided to tweet at Ford's corporate Twitter account. It couldn't hurt.

However, she was completely unprepared for what happened next: Ford tweeted back, offering to do what it could to help.

"I was so surprised when Ford's customer service team tweeted back to me," Janelle says.

And help they did. Within weeks, Janelle had her silver Fiesta, which she promptly named Feliz—Spanish for "happy."

Ford was exercising the tenets of the participation economy model. The motor company's *interaction* with Janelle via Twitter and the very *personal gesture* of locating and getting her the car of her dreams gained a Ford fan and brand evangelist for life.

"[Ford's] efforts to help me speak miles about the brand. I was very impressed," says Janelle. "I will never choose another car brand!"

And, of course, these sentiments have been duly shared online with her thousands of friends and followers.

Birth of the "Digital Native"

Considering what our research found, we aren't completely surprised by the emergence of the participation economy and illustrative stories like Janelle's that have emerged.

While non-Millennials spend roughly the same amount of time online, Millennials are more likely to use the Internet as a platform to broadcast their thoughts and experiences, and to contribute user-generated content. As described in Figure 1-6,

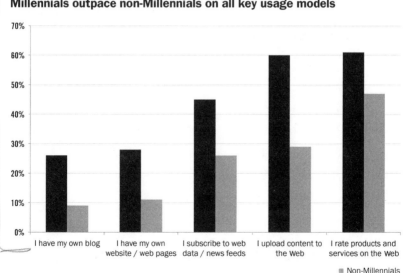

MILLENNIALS CONTRIBUTE AND CONSUME MORE WEB CONTENT

Millennials outpace non-Millennials on all key usage models

Source: Barkley, The Boston Consulting Group, and Service Management Group, "American Millennials: Deciphering the Enigma Generation," September 2011.

Figure 1-6 Millennial production and consumption of online content.

Millennials are significantly more engaged in rating products and services (60 percent vs. 46 percent of non-Millennials) and uploading videos, images, and blog entries to the Web (60 percent vs. 29 percent).

This desire to have a voice stems from the fact that Millennials are, as the writer and education authority Mark Prensky described them in 2001, "digital natives,"[9] born into a world filled with technological advances and new devices that empower the consumer. Unlike older generations, digital natives have been speaking the digital language as long as they can remember. Studies on their digital device and social media usage habits back this up. Indeed, according to an MPA and GfK MRI benchmark study on social media, among 18- to 34-year olds, social media and digital device penetration is at its highest among this demographic, with 91 percent using Facebook and 80 percent owning a digital device, according to an *Economist* article on the study.[10]

Because they are digital natives, says Jacqueline Anderson, Millennials don't necessarily delineate between the on- and offline worlds. "It is their view that these two worlds should blend seamlessly."

Beyond their widely recognized affinity for participating in marketing activities online, our research identified eight specific generational behaviors and attitudes that Millennials are likely to bring with them into their next life stages. We'll cover those in the following chapters.

Optimistic Despite the Roller-Coaster Economy

Starting with William Strauss and Neil Howe's groundbreaking 2000 book, *Millennials Rising*, most Millennial-focused studies have described this generation as optimistic.

But these days, brand marketers want to know what (if any) impact the Great Recession had on Millennials' optimism? Going further, how did the downturn impact them as consumers? Are they spending less? If so, will that continue?

First, let's consider the facts. It's been well documented in the media that many Millennials are struggling to find jobs after completing high school and college. According to the Pew Research Center, at least 37 percent of 18- to 29-year-olds are unemployed or out of the workforce, "the highest share among this age group in more than three decades." This doesn't bode well for consumer brands, as "research shows that young people who graduate from college in a bad economy typically suffer long-term consequences—with effects on their careers and earnings that linger as long as 15 years."[11]

Yet despite these struggles, Pew also found that about nine out of ten Millennials say that they currently have enough money or that they will eventually meet their long-term financial goals. There's that optimism! And why shouldn't they be optimistic? Millennials are on course to become the most educated generation in American history, thanks to the "demands of a modern knowledge-based economy." But it's also due to the fact that millions of twenty-somethings have chosen to pursue graduate degrees in part because they can't find a job.[12]

There is also some preliminary data suggesting that the downturn has had little impact so far. According to a *Forbes* article, Millennials are currently the largest demographic purchasing new technological gadgets and fashion apparel. Even more telling, suggests the author of the article, "They even start riots outside retail malls over $200 limited-edition Air Jordan sneakers."[13] And their spending on jewelry increased 27 percent in 2011, according to American Express Business Insights.[14]

What gives? The *Forbes* author goes on to suggest several reasons Millennials are continuing to spend despite the obvious constraints they are facing, from student debt to unemployment. First of all, it's the "keeping up with the Joneses" (or should we say "Kardashians"?) phenomenon at play. Thanks to the incessant number of Facebook updates they are receiving from their friends, plus "the influx of 'just like us' reality TV personalities [who] convey that these lifestyles are achievable," Millennials are under pressure to spend in order to simply keep up with their peers.[15]

It doesn't hurt that many Millennials are used to an affluent lifestyle, with 34 percent having been raised by wealthy parents who are still willing to foot the bill, according to American Express and the Harrison Group.[16] Surveys revealed that "[s]ome 59 percent of moms pay for their Millennial child's cell phone and 53 percent of moms spend more than $5,000 per year per each adult child covering everyday expenses," according to a *Forbes* article.[17] Who knows how long this open checkbook parenting will continue?

Furthermore, not every Millennial is struggling to pay the bills. Indeed, 11.8 million Millennials ages 18 to 30 are currently living in U.S. households with annual incomes exceeding $100,000, according to an Ipsos Mendelsohn Affluent Survey cited in *Forbes*.[18]

They are also projected to take over as the largest generational segment in the luxury consumer market by 2020, according to Unity Marketing.[19] So it doesn't sound like *all* Millennials are hurting.

While the jury is still out on what ultimate impact the recession will have on the Millennial generation's future spending habits, it's pretty safe to say that Millennials are already working hard to bounce back strong.

The Millennial Mindset

We've spent most of this chapter sharing what we know to be true about Millennials from our research. But we now have a question for you to ponder before we move on: How Millennial are you?

The question refers to how Millennial culture and behavior are influencing individuals of all ages in unique and surprising ways. Unlike any before them, they are actively trying to assimilate other generations into their culture.

"Millennial culture has become mainstream as a result. I see it in my own family," says Carol Phillips, president of brand marketing firm Brand Amplitude, Millennial expert, and marketing instructor at the University of Notre Dame. "My mother was never influenced by what I listened to or wore, while my son creates my playlists."

It's not uncommon for non-Millennials to find themselves exhibiting some of the very same traits as Millennials. Whether by persuading their parents to buy an iPhone, showing them how to use Facebook and Twitter, or teaching them how to find the best deals through social media and new apps, Millennials are helping non-Millennials fit into this digital environment. Suddenly non-Millennial behavior becomes harder to discern from that of Millennials. This stems partly from the fact that older generations are adopting these characteristics in order to feel and *stay* relevant in today's workforce.

According to a 2011 poll conducted by the consulting firm Twentysomething Inc., some 85 percent of graduates will be moving back home with parents, presumably because they can't find jobs.[20] Another factor is how close (literally) Millennials are to their parents these days—much closer than older generations were to their parents, as reported in the Pew Research Center's Millennials study:

> They get along well with their parents. Looking back at their teenage years, Millennials report having had fewer spats with mom or dad than older adults say they had with their own parents when they were growing up. And now, hard times have kept a significant share of adult Millennials and their parents under the same roof. About one-in-eight older Millennials (ages 22 and older) say they've "boomeranged" back to a parent's home because of the recession.[21]

Whereas Boomers' parents were certain that the devil had arrived when Elvis's hip-swinging rock 'n' roll first hit the scene, youth culture today embodies plenty to which older generations actually aspire.

"Parenting underwent a shift in the 1980s," Phillips says. "Children became the focus of family life, going everywhere with their parents. Many of these children are supported by their parents well into their 20s," she says. "There has been a blurring of the generations thanks to this close proximity."

Through consumer research, MTV uncovered this shift several years ago, which ultimately led to significant changes in the channel's approach to programming.

"When Gen X was growing up, you didn't see parents on popular youth shows. You certainly never saw them on MTV," says Stephen Friedman, MTV president. "Suddenly, we were finding that our main audience—the Millennial-aged audience—is best friends with their parents."

The finding played a role in one of their more risky decisions: to green-light *16 and Pregnant*, a show that features the critical role parents play in helping teen children prepare to become parents. Another show that helped pave the way was *World's Strictest Parents*, which was originally pitched to MTV, but which the network turned down because it "just made more sense on sister channel CMT at the time," Friedman explains.

The show was a strong performer on CMT, and based on the new audience research, MTV decided to try rebroadcasting some of the episodes. *World's Strictest Parents* exceeded expectations and did well on MTV, providing further proof that it was OK to feature parents on a show that targeted teens. The MTV development team was working on the concept for *16 and Pregnant* at the time, and the decision was made to develop it. It quickly became one of the highest-rated shows on the channel.

"Never before would we have ever run something like that. It's a real family drama where parents are playing critical roles," says Friedman. "Never in the generation before would you have wanted to see your parents or grandparents on the show. And yet our audience—the Millennial viewer—was craving it, and they still do today."

The big takeaway here? For Millennials, it's okay, even cool, to be friends with their parents, and vice versa.

Not only are Millennials serving as leading indicators on media consumption, advocacy, and social media usage habits among other generations, but also they are indirectly influencing buying decisions to the tune of an estimated $500 billion each year. And while non-Millennials have influence over their spouses and children, thanks to their digital reach, a Millennial's ability to influence is much broader, from parents, siblings, and friends to total strangers on the Web.

The authors of this book are no exception: Jeff regularly seeks advice from his three children—twins Laura and Abby, 21, and Scott, 16. When the family buys electronics, smartphones, or even a subscription service like Netflix, for instance, his kids are quickly able to share the pros and cons of the various brands or purchase plans. They have strong, fact-based points of view because they have grown up using technology every single day. And Christie, a Millennial, regularly gives advice to her parents on such issues.

To sum up, a Millennial mindset has taken hold of American culture, radiating beyond the Millennial generation to older generations, and there is no going back.

The takeaway for marketers? To predict what will be hot tomorrow, you merely need to look to what's hot with Millennials today.

So where do we go from here? Outside of a weeklong trip to the Williamsburg Greenpoint neighborhood in Brooklyn (a hotbed of Millennial culture), it's time for a new set of rules for Marketing to Millennials.

CHAPTER 1: **KEY TAKEAWAYS**

▸ **Millennials want to participate.** Not willing to just be passive consumers any longer, this generation wants to actively participate, cocreate, and be included as partners in the brands they love.

▸ **Millennials are heavily influenced by their peers.** Most Millennial consumers turn to friends before making a purchase decision.

▸ **Millennials have more friends.** Not only are Millennials heavily influenced by their peers, but they have increasingly larger networks of friends they can share ideas with and receive feedback from.

▸ **Millennials are digital natives.** Born into an era when smartphones are abundant and texting is a fixture in communication, Millennials fluently speak the digital language.

▸ **A millennial mindset has overtaken popular culture.** To know what will be hot with American consumers tomorrow, look to what is popular among Millennials today.

The New Rules of Marketing to Millennials

The Holy Grail for many marketers today? To create a timeless brand that can speak to all consumers, regardless of their life stage or generation.

But the question of "how" is tricky. One merely needs to consider prevailing market research to know that, from core values to modes of expression, generations are fundamentally different and, correspondingly, their purchasing decisions are vastly different.

Multigenerational marketing has been an effective strategy for dealing with these differences. By targeting generational groups with promotional messages and products that reflect their generational values, marketers can drive their target's consumption behavior.

We already know a lot about the Baby Boomers, who have been the predominant cultural influencer for decades. Next on the scene were the Gen Xers, who have also been analyzed for years.

Today, we are witnessing the emerging influence of the Millennials. And yet, despite this influence, we are only just beginning to understand them as active consumers who are interested in participating in the marketing process.

The "What" Generation?

Call them the Millennials or Gen Y, we just can't seem to settle on a name, as noted in a Havas Worldwide, *Prosumer Report*:

> Since the century's start, we've heard a profusion of terms used to describe the generation born between the mid-1980s and early 2000s: *digital natives*, coined by Mark Prensky to emphasize their break from the analogue generations that had gone before; *Millennials*, to designate them as children of the new millennium; *gen Y*, to indicate they followed gen X, or *gen why*, in a nod to their questioning natures; *echo boomers*, to underscore their large numbers; and so on.[1]

In a follow-up to our survey, "American Millennials: Deciphering the Enigma Generation," BCG asked Millennials and non-Millennials to come up with words that best described the generation. Survey participants, too, had difficulty choosing one word, as illustrated in the word-cloud graphics in Figures 2-1 and 2-2.

BCG's research revealed a high degree of consistency in how non-Millennials view Millennials, while Millennials' perceptions of themselves are more fragmented. Also note that there is little overlap between the two viewpoints, indicating that powerful stereotypes could be preventing companies from acknowledging the diversity of the Millennial generation and color their views of Millennial consumers overall.

In other words, "companies could be investing time and resources into ineffective, inauthentic, and not resonant mar-

Source: BCG Analysis.

Figure 2-1 How Millennials perceive themselves.
(The size of the word in the cloud indicates the frequency
with which it was used in free-text responses.)

keting campaigns that don't reach the intended target audience
member," Christine Barton, partner and managing director at
BCG and coauthor of the research study, says. Don't let that
be you.

Source: BCG Analysis.

Figure 2-2 How non-Millennials perceive Millennials. (The size of the word
indicates the frequency with which it was used in free-text responses.)

An Enigma Generation?

The subtitle of our study is "Deciphering the Enigma Generation," but are Millennials really an enigma? As long as you understand the key differences, they don't have to be. In fact, this generation is more straightforward than any previous generation. You just have to be willing to spend time with them.

Jacqueline Anderson, whom you met in Chapter 1, elaborates: "If the brand marketer is not immersed in youth culture or take time to understand the Millennial mindset, [he or she] will be baffled by this group. The good news is, if you spend a little time getting to know them, the rewards will be tenfold."

This book is all about helping you get to know this generation. Our first tip? Get an Xbox and start a new bad habit. At least that's what Rudy Wilson, former vice president of marketing and brand leader of Frito-Lay, did. While the thought of a senior brand marketer playing Xbox each day might make you chuckle, Wilson insisted this was serious (and, yes, fun) work!

"Everyone feels like they can market to Millennials because they were a teen at one time," says Wilson. "But this teen is very different. Sure, there is a ton of research out there, but to really understand the generation you have to spend time with them."

Realizing how important Millennials were to the Doritos, Cheetos, SunChips, and Fritos brands he managed at the time, not only did Wilson have his team playing Xbox each week *at work,* but he also had them frequenting local Millennial-favorite clubs in Dallas, where Frito-Lay is headquartered. What's more, he had them create weekly "cultural scorecards" to keep track of the hottest new trends among members of the generation. What topped the Billboard Hot 100 chart for a particular week? Rudy's team knew!

identify target and interact w/them

Anthropologists call this approach "experimental ethnography"—qualitative research that explores a particular group's cultural phenomena.[2] In layperson's terms, you have to do exactly what Wilson and his team did: get inside the heads of your target consumers by engaging and interacting with them (even if that means losing an Xbox game or two).

"I was playing Xbox Live with the Doritos logo as my picture one time, competing with players around the world. I was losing really bad," recalls Wilson. "This one young kid, probably 10 or 11, had some choice words for me, something to the effect: 'Crunch on that Mr. Dorito!' I had to laugh."

To help you crack the code on Millennials as consumers (beyond playing your favorite Xbox game), our research identified several common Millennial behaviors and attitudes that the generation is likely to bring into their future life stages such as marriage and parenthood. This book covers those that are of importance to the majority of brands, whether consumer packaged goods, restaurant, or retail. These attributes will not change over time; thus, they form the basis of our new rules of Marketing to Millennials—marketing tactics that work when it comes to engaging this new generation of consumers.

Here's a quick overview of the rules we'll be covering in the following chapters:

- Engage these early adopters of new technologies and emerging social tools.

- Build a listening and participation strategy that will help you connect with your brand advocates.

- Make them look good among their peers.

- Design a sense of adventure and fun into your brand experience.

- Keep their loyalty by giving them no reason to cheat on you.

Before diving in, let's spend some time on a few elements that are essential to understanding our research on the Millennial consumer.

Begin a Relationship Now, If You Haven't Already

Several of the Millennial marketing examples you'll read in this book come from start-ups or brands that launched with Millennials as a primary target audience. Easy for them to successfully target this market—right?

So what does this mean for well-established brands that have long marketed to older generations? Can they use the same tactics to gain traction with the Millennial consumer?

Our friend and coauthor of our research, Christine Barton, partner at BCG, has some interesting thoughts on the challenge: "It's easier as a startup, as you're not risking anything and just growing with the tail winds behind you. It's really hard for most companies to start putting capital and management time into going after the millennial market," she says. "For companies whose core focus is on Boomers, often the thought is, 'Why would you, as there is still growth with that generation?'"

However, given their size and influence, you can't afford to ignore the need to begin building relationships with Millennials—your future target consumers. The sooner you do, the better.

"If you don't put the work in now to get to know this consumer, you won't be able to know them in three to five to eight years when you really need to begin worrying about them," says Barton. "You start by doing credible consumer research—qualitative as well as quantitative—and then segment results. Millennials are not monolithic."

The advantage to starting today is that those companies that truly "get" this generation will have an opportunity to differentiate themselves and forge profitable long-term relationships with Millennial consumers.

Once you have a better understanding of the segments that are most relevant to the future of your brand through consumer research, it's time to start the brand introduction, conversation, and engagement.

"It's about getting that timing right so you're not too far ahead of the return but that you're not investing too late," says Barton. "It's harder to be authentic and credible if you invest in them too late."

Begin allocating part of your budget to Millennial-specific marketing, messaging, and media. At some point, however, you'll need to start laying in the products and services, Barton rightly warns.

"You can't just message to them forever without beginning to deliver against them," she says. "Do you develop a brand and grow it as a core or do you add to your portfolio of preexisting brands? These are complex strategic issues that companies will have to face when it comes to resource allocation."

But proceed with caution. The risk here is the negative impact it could have on the core brand. The potential payoff is worth it, however, which is why Macy's recently committed to winning over this generation, as you'll learn in the following case study.

CASE STUDY: Retailer Aims to Attract Next Generation of Consumers

Who?   Macy's

What?   After learning, through company
                  research, that Macy's is not
                  "the store of choice" for older
                  Millennials, the retailer announced
                  plans in 2012 to implement a
                  "Millennial strategy."

How?   The Millennial strategy is being
                  rolled out in phases over three years,
                  including enhancing its fashion
                  assortment and shopping experience
                  in mstylelab (targeted for 13- to 22-
                  year-olds) and Impulse (for 19- to
                  30-year-olds).

"We believe we have great opportunity to accelerate sales growth among customers in this generation," said Jeffrey Gennette, Macy's chief merchandising officer, in a statement.[3] "Doing so requires us to think from the customer's point of view about our assortments and store experience, and to align our internal resources so we can move quickly and with focus. The Millennial strategy is a natural extension of Macy's very successful work over the past three years in developing My Macy's localization, omnichannel integration, and customer engagement through MAGIC Selling."

Companies, such as Macy's, that start testing the waters today in order to truly get to know the Millennial generation have an opportunity to differentiate themselves and forge profitable long-term relationships with these influential consumers.

Younger and Older Millennials: A Difference?

In our study, we extended the definition of Millennials by about four to five years beyond what is commonly considered the typical Millennial age range. Why? We wanted to find out what impact marriage, structured jobs, higher discretionary incomes, and kids would have on their consumption habits. Basically, we wanted to know what differences, if any, existed between younger and older Millennials.

So what did we find? Well, first, you have to understand the difference between a life stage and a generational characteristic. Imagine that you are 18 again and haven't a care in the world. You recently graduated from high school, and you have some time before starting college or a job.

A friend calls you one day and invites you to join her on a once-in-a-lifetime trip to an exotic location in South Africa. It's an expensive trip, sure, but since you have enough money saved to cover it, what better time to go?

With this thought in mind, you hop online the next day to book your trip.

Now let's change this scenario. Imagine that you have a two-year-old child at home and a spouse who is not so eager for you to leave him at home alone with full-time parental duties. Suddenly, that exotic trip doesn't seem like such an easy thing to manage, so you decide to decline the invitation.

The point of this example is to make the distinction between a life stage and a generational characteristic. Here, the ability to "live in the moment" and accept a last-minute invitation to travel to South Africa is a life stage characteristic that our research found is common to Millennials. But it's a characteristic that is likely to fall away once they start having children.

Our research identified a significant difference between younger and older Millennials: While younger Millennials express a desire to give to global causes, once they start having kids they enter a life stage that's focused more on giving locally and effecting local change—almost a narrowing of perspective.

Another interesting area to explore is the impact of the recent economic downturn on the behaviors and habits of older and younger Millennials. The older Millennials, who entered the labor market during the most recent economic expansion, in 2002–07, found a relatively healthy economy with many job options. If they were fortunate enough to keep their jobs, they have continued to develop skills and accumulate experience and wealth that enables them to put further distance between them- . selves and others who have been less fortunate.

On the other hand, younger Millennials, who graduated from college beginning in 2008, faced a slow economy with few to no job opportunities. This stark reality will most certainly have some kind of impact. As one blogger put it, "At the end of the day, the distinguishing feature of recessions is that they create winners and losers within each generation. It is the differences between those thrown out of work versus those who keep their jobs that are more important defining features of labor market experience than generational."[4]

However, generational characteristics—those that are common to members of a particular generation despite life stage differences—should not change over time. For instance, our study found that a majority of Millennials are early adopters of technology; even those with children continue to adopt new technology with enthusiasm. This is a generational rather than a life stage characteristic.

The rest of this book focuses on these generational characteristics and how companies can build marketing strategies that tap these insights.

Six Distinct Millennial Segments

Before moving on, there is one last item to highlight. Despite the common characteristics and seemingly overarching stereotypes that our research identified, Millennials are by no means a homogeneous group. Like all populations, Millennials can be segmented into unique and specific subgroups.

By looking at their responses to questions on technology, cause marketing, and general outlook on life, our research partners at BCG identified six distinct segments within the Millennial population that we wrote about in "The Millennial Consumer: Debunking Stereotypes."[5] These segments include: Hip-ennial, Old-School Millennial, Gadget Guru, Clean and Green Millennial, Millennial Mom, and Anti-Millennial. Each of these segments, detailed in the persona descriptions that follow, exhibit Millennial traits in varying degrees and combinations.

Millennial Personas: A Segmentation Model

Hip-ennial: Cautious, Global, Charitable, and Information Hungry

Hip-ennial

"I can make the world a better place."

- Cautious consumer, global, charitable, and information hungry
- Greatest user of social media, but does not push/contribute content; looking for entertainment
- Female dominated, below average employment due to students and homemakers

29%

Source: BCG analysis, Barkley expression of BCG analysis.

Heather, a 24-year-old art major at the University of California, Santa Cruz, has a bright and hopeful view of the world. True, the current job market stinks and there's a giant question mark hanging over her life after graduation, but she dreams of a successful future. Her work on the Obama presidential campaign helped solidify her idealistic point of view, and she honestly believes the different religions and cultures of the world can someday peacefully coexist. She has grand plans for international travel, and while she has yet to obtain a passport, she loves to research the different continents she'll one day visit.

This Saturday, she and her friends are eating lunch at the hot spot Charlie Hong Kong before heading over to American Apparel for some new T-shirts. Heather has spent a great deal of time online researching the best ones, and she loves that American Apparel manufactures everything in the United States, adhering to strong environmental policies. She doesn't mind spending a little more on products from such a cause-minded company. She's a "fan" of them on Facebook, along with the Bill & Melinda Gates Foundation.

Overall, she shops most frequently for clothing at Walmart but hopes to get a job after college that will pay enough for her to shop more at Gap, American Eagle Outfitters, and Victoria's Secret.

Throughout the day she'll check in with Facebook and post pictures of herself and her friends that she took with her iPhone.

She'll also check her LinkedIn account, as she's trying to fire up her job search efforts. Tonight, when she's winding down, she'll put on her Gap RED sweatshirt, turn on some acoustic music, and go on her iPad to check out a funny YouTube link her friend e-mailed her earlier that day. She'll also text her friends to remind them of the Susan G. Komen Race for the Cure they're doing next Saturday.

Old-School Millennial: Disconnected, Cautious, and Charitable

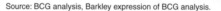

Old-School Millennial

"Connecting on Facebook is too impersonal, let's meet up for coffee instead!"

- Disconnected, cautious consumer, and charitable
- Confident, independent, and self-directed
- Spends least amount of time online in most activities; reads printed media
- Above-average Hispanic, a little older

10%

Source: BCG analysis, Barkley expression of BCG analysis.

Roberto is a 30-year-old life insurance sales associate at Prudential. He earns a decent salary and is good at what he does, conducting in-depth research to find the best policies for his clients. In fact, seeking out information is what he does best. This weekend he plans to purchase a new flat-screen television for his bedroom. He plans to visit Best Buy and Costco to check prices and talk to sales associates about whether plasma or LCD would be the better way to go. He wants to understand why some televisions are better than others and why some are more reliable in the long term. He knows he could research all of this online, but he gets frustrated with conflicting product reviews on the Internet and would rather just talk to someone in person. Besides, he uses the Internet more for online magazines like *GQ* and *Men's Health,* or for weather updates and maps from MapQuest. He's not into social media outlets like Facebook. As far as he's concerned, they're a waste of time. Every now and then he'll shop online from a trusted retailer like JCPenney .com, but more often than not he'll just go to the store itself.

When he arrives at Best Buy, he begins looking at television brands he knows and trusts. He discovers Samsung's cause-marketing effort "Team Up for Autism." This resonates with him, since his nephew was recently diagnosed with the disorder. He decides to limit his choice to one of Samsung's televisions to help support the cause. If it costs a little more, so be it. His friends suggested checking the Internet for better deals, but he's not comfortable giving out his personal information online. He'll just go ahead and buy it in the store. Overall, he sees many problems in the world today and thinks that everyone should purchase products that support a cause.

Gadget Guru: Successful, Wired, and Free-Spirited

Gadget Guru

"It's a great day to be me."

- Successful, wired and free-spirited, confident, at ease
- Now is his best decade
- Greatest device ownership, pushes/contributes to content
- Male dominated, above-average income, more single

13%

Source: BCG analysis, Barkley expression of BCG analysis.

James is a 25-year-old "work hard/play hard" kind of guy. He's a software developer at Google and loves his job, mainly because of the supercool vibe and hip coworkers. He's a free spirit who believes now is the time of his life. He's totally confident the world is his oyster and wants to protect it by using environmentally friendly products. Always one to carry the hottest device, he'll buy the newest version the second it comes out. He recently bought the latest iPhone and an HD widescreen video camera. He carries an iPad and a Kindle as well.

Tonight he'll leave work at 7:30 and flip on the TomTom GPS in his Toyota Prius to find the closest GNC that's open until 9:00. He'll swing by and pick up more of the omega-3 supplements and multivitamins he's recently run out of, as he wants to keep his body as healthy as possible. When he gets home he'll whip up a quick stir-fry using the fresh organic vegetables he picked up at the store yesterday, then he'll spend an hour on his MacBook Air blogging and updating his website with content. He'll scan *Wired* and *Fast Company* online, check a few news feeds and blogs to keep up with the latest trends, and then spend some time in an online software forum on LinkedIn.

Finally, choosing between his Xbox and Playstation 3, he'll settle into a night of gaming with Call of Duty. He'll stay up all night playing against some guy in Germany (talking to him on a headset, of course) and roll into work an hour late the next day.

> ### Clean and Green Millennial: Impressionable, Cause Driven, Healthy, and Green

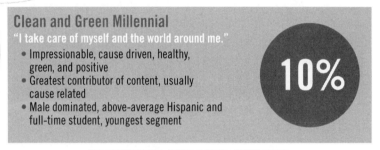

Clean and Green Millennial
"I take care of myself and the world around me."
- Impressionable, cause driven, healthy, green, and positive
- Greatest contributor of content, usually cause related
- Male dominated, above-average Hispanic and full-time student, youngest segment

10%

Source: BCG analysis, Barkley expression of BCG analysis.

Marcus is an adventurous, 24-year-old Hispanic grad student at the University of Colorado in Boulder. He loves living in the mountains and spends a lot of time outdoors, backcountry snowboarding, hiking, and mountain biking with his friends.

As far as grad school goes, you could say he's trying to "do it all" on that front, too. He's switched majors three times and is now focusing on the entertainment industry. He'd love to do something really off the wall, but the solicited advice from his friends and family still hasn't helped him figure out what that might be. Honestly, he's fine with the lack of direction in his life. He's having a blast with the way things are right now, enjoying a part-time job that pays him well and suits his current lifestyle perfectly.

This weekend he's running a fundraiser for the Boulder Alzheimer's Walk taking place next month. This will be his third year volunteering, and he's managed to get a lot of friends to help out. He's hoping to top last year's donations.

Everyone who knows Marcus considers him "lean and green" and a bit of a loner. He's a health nut and eats only nutrition-rich foods. He shops weekly at the local farmers market and eats regularly at Black Cat Farm–Table–Bistro. He believes passionately in their philosophy of farm-to-table food. While he's not big into working out (he's too busy with school and outdoor pursuits), he does take the time to read the nutritional contents of foods to make sure he's eating right.

When it comes to the environment, Marcus bikes to school to reduce his carbon footprint and seeks out products with environmentally friendly policies, such as Kellogg's. He's very vocal about his green efforts and blogs about them regularly. While he's not online as much as his friends, he reads online magazine and news reports on green efforts and frequently uploads articles and videos that help support his opinions. He'd go so far as to call himself a "green expert."

He wouldn't define himself as "crunchy." In fact, style matters to him. After school he plans to shop online at Express and Aeropostale. He got an e-mail about big sales going on at both stores, and he loves a good deal. (You should see the number of frequent shopper cards in his wallet.)

Millennial "Mom": Wealthy, Family-Oriented, and Digitally Savvy

Millennial "Mom"
"I love to work out, travel, and pamper my baby."

- Wealthy, family-oriented, works out, confident, and digitally savvy
- High online intensity in terms of time, activities, and shopping
- Highly social
- Female dominated, a little older, highest income of segments; above-average Hispanic share

22%

Source: BCG analysis, Barkley expression of BCG analysis.

Amy is an independent and outgoing 28-year-old mother of a toddler. She's an "on-the-go" and "in-the-know" kind of mom who thinks of herself as young and hip. In her mind, having a child hasn't changed a thing. She spends a ton of time and money making sure she and her daughter have the best of everything. She loves her job as a brand manager at Procter & Gamble, where she pulls down a great salary that helps support her love affair with online shopping.

Three to four times a week she jogs three miles with her Nike pedometer, later uploading her results to her Nike iPhone app. If it's raining, she'll do an hour of Wii Fit before heading in to the office. A few times a month she'll take her daughter to Mommy Yoga on Saturday mornings.

At work, Amy will use her iPad to check out the mommy blog Suburbanturmoil.com, which she finds hilarious. Since her daughter is nearing kindergarten age (which happened so fast!), she'll also research local elementary schools to find the best in her district. Of course, she'll update her status on Facebook and check out the latest posts and pictures from her friends. She'll take a minute to upload that funny picture of her daughter in the leaf pile, too. Every Friday on her lunch break she uses her iPhone to book dinner reservations through opentable.com for date night with her husband. She loves trying different ethnic restaurants around town. When she wants live music (Adele, for example), she'll buy tickets through Ticketmaster.com.

After church on Sunday, Amy goes online to research recipes for next week's dinners. She'll also double-check her Huggies situation to determine whether she needs to order more through Diapers.com.

Since she's throwing a third birthday party for her daughter in a few weeks, she'll shop for children's party dresses at Gap.com and ChildrensPlace.com. She already checked out Zulily and Etsy for something special but didn't find anything she loved. Of course, she wants to look her best, too, so she'll order a new cashmere sweater from Anthropologie.com and a pair of heels from Zappos to wear to the party.

She and her husband have blocked off a week's vacation in the spring, so she goes online to research different destinations. She's thinking Italy or the Dominican Republic. Both cultures seem intriguing. She'd love to take a bike tour through Tuscany (with her daughter on the back, of course), and there's a wilderness dude ranch in Jarabacoa that sounds amazing. She'll check Orbitz.com and Travelocity.com for fares, plus she'll monitor FareCompare on her iPhone.

In the evenings, after putting her daughter to bed, she'll either read a book on Kindle or she and her husband will watch a recorded show on TiVo.

Anti-Millennial: Locally Minded and Conservative

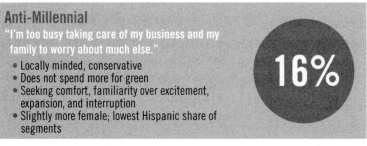

Anti-Millennial

"I'm too busy taking care of my business and my family to worry about much else."

- Locally minded, conservative
- Does not spend more for green
- Seeking comfort, familiarity over excitement, expansion, and interruption
- Slightly more female; lowest Hispanic share of segments

16%

Source: BCG analysis, Barkley expression of BCG analysis.

Danielle loves to bake. She's a 27-year-old African-American who owns a little pie shop in Tulsa, Oklahoma. With a dream and her grandmother's sweet potato pie recipe, she built the shop entirely on her own after her divorce three years ago. It hasn't been easy, but she's proud of the pie shop's success. It's given her freedom and the money to buy a house for herself and her five-year-old son.

Being an entrepreneur has been challenging. With two full-time employees and the threat of higher taxes and new healthcare mandates for small businesses, she's stressed about making ends meet. She thinks big government should just back off and let free markets do their thing. In her opinion, the current government meddles too much and spends an outrageous amount of money. She can't believe the out-of-control state of the U.S. budget.

She's definitely not into the whole trendy "green" movement. For starters, she can't afford to buy organic and doesn't really believe it makes much of a difference in the end. She shops at Albertsons and sticks to ingredients that are on sale or are relatively inexpensive. She never researches her products before she buys them, and she certainly never buys something because it's linked to a charity. That's just a ploy to get her to spend more of her hard-earned money. She doesn't have time to recycle, and she drives a 2000 Chevy Tahoe because it's great for making pie deliveries. At the shop, she serves her "to-go" coffee in Styrofoam cups.

She's very careful with her money and does her back-to-school shopping at Walmart and Kohl's. She's not all that interested in traveling but is considering a drive to the World Aquarium in Dallas with her son over his spring break.

When it comes to the Internet, she prefers social media outlets and entertainment sites. She likes Facebook, mainly because it allows her to keep up with her church activities and her friends. She likes to comment on their pictures and posts. She'll post from time to time herself, usually about something funny her son said. On slow days at the shop she'll check out People.com or Popsugar.com on her iPhone to catch up on celebrity gossip.

It is critical for brands seeking to engage this new generation of consumers to know which of these Millennial segments is most important to their brand and category.

"Otherwise, if the brand tries to go after the entire monolithic group at once, it could end up doing something that does not appeal or is at cross-purposes to a key segment," explains Christine Barton, partner at BCG. "Instead, brands should optimize their relationship with their key targets with whom their brand has permission."

As we're about to see, the same applies to dealing with gender differences.

Millennial Guys and Gals

As our segmentation explicitly points out, Millennials are *not* all alike, especially when it comes to the sexes. Indeed, some of the key differences between Millennial men and women are their lifestyle and purchase behaviors. But before we dive into that, let's spend a little time parsing some key statistics.

According to the Bureau of Labor Statistics, women now earn 60 percent of master's degrees, about half of all law and medical degrees, and 42 percent of MBAs. In the workplace, women have also made strides, now holding 51.4 percent of managerial and professional jobs—up from 26.1 percent in 1980. And in the professional fields, close to one-third of America's physicians are now women, as are 45 percent of associates in law firms.[6]

Despite these advances, women continue to face barriers. Pay equity is a key concern. Fifty years after the Equal Pay Act, women are still paid an average of 77 cents for every dollar paid to men. Our study backs this up: Millennial men report higher discretionary income than women across different age groups and races. Only 2.6 percent of companies in the Fortune 500 are led by a female CEO. A mere 15.2 percent of board seats are occupied by women. And at the country's top 100 law firms, only 17 percent of equity partners are women.[7]

While these barriers to women's advancement in the workplace and society impact their overall consumption behaviors, studies show that women are wielding more power in the household than ever before and will continue to do so as more Millennials come of age, get married, and have children.

According to a Havas Worldwide, *Prosumer Report,* on gender differences between Millennial men and women, where "couples once were 'man and wife,' now they are full-fledged partners, sharing resources and responsibilities as they work toward common goals. It is marriage as merger." With this more equal footing, however, women are finding themselves in the position of being the " 'deciders' in some important respects," as opposed to the past, when men were the heads of the household who claimed ownership of major household decisions. Today, women, especially mothers, are "calling the shots" when a situation involves major household purchase decisions.[8]

Indeed, a Pew Research Center survey found that the woman makes decisions in more areas than the man in 43 percent of all couples. Men make more of the decisions in only 26 percent of all couples, while couples that split the decision-making responsibilities comprise the remaining 31 percent.[9]

"Mothers are now directly influencing the spend for a family unit," says Christine Barton, partner at BCG. "Not surprisingly, there is a lot of consumption of mom opinions thanks to an overwhelming number of mothers, especially first-time moms, turning to social media for product research and advice. There is a tremendous amount of power in mom advocacy as a unit."

So what does all this mean for brand marketers? For one thing, gender distinctions are no longer set in stone, as the Havas Worldwide, *Prosumer Report*, points out: "The NFL is targeting women. Men are enjoying herbal wraps at their local day spa. It only makes sense to move away from 'either/or' in favor of 'and.' "[10]

In terms of consumption habits, our study unequivocally found that gender affects Millennial spending, with women spending disproportionately on apparel and men on automotive. Millennial men spend more than Millennial women on consumer retail (16 percent vs. 11 percent), while Millennial women spend more than Millennial men on apparel (33 percent vs. 22 percent).

Given these differences, it "makes sense to think of millennial men and women as two different cohort groups," says Carol Phillips, president of Brand Amplitude, Millennial expert, and marketing instructor at the University of Notre Dame, says.

We have to agree. Spend time getting to know your target consumers and the differences, whether by segment or by gender. But before you can even begin that process, you'll need a basic understanding of what makes Millennial consumers tick.

That's what this book is all about. So let's get started with the new rules of Marketing to Millennials.

CHAPTER 2: **KEY TAKEAWAYS**

- ▶ **Multigenerational marketing proves vital for brand success with Millennials.** Ignoring the varying purchase behavior between Millennials and non-Millennials can be severely damaging for brands. Understanding your audience will inevitably help drive success with Millennials, as they require different marketing than other generations.

- ▶ **Non-Millennials are more likely to stereotype Millennials.** There is a high degree of consistency in how non-Millennials view Millennials, while Millennials' perceptions of themselves are more fragmented. Thus, powerful stereotypes could be preventing companies from acknowledging the diversity of the Millennial generation, leading them to invest and put resources into ineffective and embarrassing marketing campaigns that don't reach the intended target audience member.

- ▶ **Millennials don't have to be enigmas.** Spend time with Millennials and you will see they are more straightforward than you once realized. Follow in the footsteps of progressive brand thought leaders and live life like a Millennial. The answer isn't necessarily found in numbers but in simply spending time in the Millennial world.

- ▶ **Millennials have several specific behaviors and attitudes in common.** These generational characteristics are the ones they are likely to bring into their next life stage and, thus, form the basis of our new rules of Marketing to Millennials—marketing tactics that work when it comes to engaging this new generation of consumer.

> ➤ **But not all Millennials are alike.** Millennials are not a homogeneous group. Like all populations, they can be segmented into unique and specific subgroups. Brands should seek to optimize their relationship with their key targets.

CHAPTER 3

Engage These Early Adopters of New Technologies

I love keeping up with the latest tech and media trends on Facebook or Twitter, concerning start-ups, new networks, new gadgets. I owned the first generation iPhone and will likely continue to own future generations of the iPhone. If I weren't a poor student, I'd own more products. My next acquisition will either be the Fitbit or the Basis band, both of which are healthcare monitoring devices.

—Megan L., 27, Philadelphia, Pennsylvania

We all know that devices are not what they used to be. A phone is no longer just a phone. An MP3 player now can connect to the Internet and act as a game device. The functionality of almost any given device overlaps with that of other devices.

Along with these nifty new tech products comes the age-old question: Do I really *need* to upgrade?

For older generations, the thought process is usually something like this: "If my phone works, why would I need a new one?" For Millennials like Megan, if the functions on the new phone are worth spending money on, there is no question. They have to have it!

This is a fundamental difference between generations, stemming from the fact that Millennials are 2.5 times more likely to be early adopters, or the first to test the latest and greatest new technology. In fact, 56 percent of Millennials report that they are usually among the first to try a new technology. See Figure 3-1.

MILLENNIALS MORE LIKELY TO ADOPT NEW TECHNOLOGY
Millennials 2.5x more likely to be an early adopter

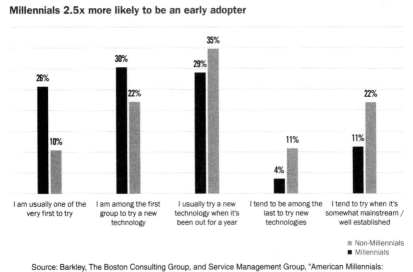

Source: Barkley, The Boston Consulting Group, and Service Management Group, "American Millennials: Deciphering the Enigma Generation," September 2011.

Figure 3-1 Millennials are digital natives.

Having to purchase something new every six months doesn't faze them in the least. They don't worry about what features will be available six months from now because there will be an even more powerful device available twelve months from now, when they can afford to upgrade. In fact, in some cases, brands have tapped these consumers to contribute to the upgrade development process itself.

Contrast this with non-Millennials: Thirty-five percent usually wait a year before trying a new technology, while 22 percent admit that they wait until a technology is well established before they take the leap.

Given this finding, it comes as no surprise that Millennials have an enormous influence over members of the older generation, who seek counsel from these young tech experts. As we'll see in the next section, this distinguishing Millennial characteristic—their early-adopter nature—presents an interesting opportunity for marketers who can figure out how to reach these young influencers.

The Household CTO

❝ I am constantly learning and adapting to new technology. Although I do not consider myself exceptional, older people are constantly making remarks about my computer and software skills. My own mother often asks me to help her by fixing the printer, reconnecting to the Internet or performing a task in Microsoft Word. She always seems amazed that I'm such a 'tech wizard,' but really it is just second nature to me. Also, at my place of employment, some of the older people in management refer to me as a computer geek because I can adapt so quickly to new technology and software.❞

—Mike, 23, Indianapolis, Indiana

Does Mike sound familiar? Come on, admit it. If you're not a Millennial, you've likely asked one—a friend, coworker, or family member—for tech assistance. And if you are a Millennial, you've likely provided such help.

"Millennials are the chief technology officers in most households these days," says Brand Amplitude's Carol Phillips. "Not only are they helping their parents troubleshoot tech problems, they're making a lot of technology decisions in households across America, directly impacting what their parents end up buying."

Like many Millennials his age, Mike recently moved back home after college to save money. Luckily, he's very close to his parents (another common trait among Millennials), and while at first blush it sounds like he's getting the better end of the deal (free rent!), he's wearing the family's CTO hat, helping his parents make savvier purchase decisions. They all seem to think it's a pretty fair trade.

"My parents recently wanted to get a projector but didn't have a clue which brand to go with," says Mike. "So I got on CNET [a popular tech product review website] to see what products had the highest ratings because it helps to know what customers think about products. After a few hours of looking around, Blue-ray [Projector] was the clear winner."

His parents agreed, and now the entire family (younger siblings included) is enjoying the purchase. A similar story line can be found in Jeff's family. Recently, his son Scott, 16, born just a year after the Millennial range we studied, commandeered Jeff's new iPad to show him how to set up notifications, narrow in on news that's more interesting, and even find some cool apps to add to his desktop.

The moral of these stories? While Millennials like Mike might not be opening their own wallets for these purchases (our research suggests that parents are likely to shell out the money for their kids' devices), they are definitely influencing what their family members—and even their coworkers—decide to buy. And their ability to influence older generations isn't limited to technology. It's impacting purchasing decisions across a wide range of product categories. Indeed, according to recent research, Millennials are influencing purchasing decisions to the tune of $500 billion each year!

Let's pause on this point, as it presents an interesting opportunity and challenge for companies from a brand messaging perspective. Currently, significant market research goes into how a message is received and understood by the primary target audience.

But children are now influencing parents to open their wallets for major purchase decisions. Given this shift of influence, marketers need to think about how their message will be conveyed by the primary target (the Millennial) to the secondary target (his or her parents). No longer is it merely about how their primary target reacts to the message. After all, if parents are ultimately the ones whipping out the credit card for these purchases, it's important to know (and be able to influence) how Millennial children are carrying and translating that brand message.

I Know More Than My CEO

Speaking of the Millennial generation's influence in the workplace, meet Elizabeth, 27. A communications manager at a major nonprofit with headquarters in Chicago, she has found herself in the position of being the organization's go-to social media expert.

When Facebook's Timeline format launched, many of her older colleagues were "freaking out," so Elizabeth stepped in to help decide which photos and milestones they should use on their cover page.

"Social media is truly a foreign language for several of my older colleagues on staff. [Millennials] seem to be more comfortable with the idea of trying something to see if it works, and if it doesn't, trying something else," says Elizabeth. "Members [of older generations] want exact dimensions, but these things generally don't come with an instruction booklet!"

Thanks to her expertise and willingness to try to implement new things, Elizabeth has reaped many professional benefits.

"At this point in my career, it's rare to be an expert and to know more than my CEO [about a particular aspect of the company]," says Elizabeth. "I get to participate in board meetings and enjoy opportunities that otherwise would have been closed off to me for many years. Something that comes so easy to me has been a door opener."

You don't have to look far to find similar examples. In fact, you likely have a few Millennials like Elizabeth walking the halls of your company. Millennials feel they *should* be rewarded for being smart and doing things well, which is not based on the number of years one has spent with a company, explains Jacqueline Anderson, of J.D. Power and Associates, whom you met in Chapter 1.

"This is an important aspect of working with Millennials not just in the workplace but also in the co-creation process. They don't necessarily regard hierarchies the same way other generations do, and that's why the power of this younger generation is so strong," says Anderson. "This extra knowledge doesn't come from years of on-the-job experience but by growing up and living in the world we live in."

MTV recognized the need to tap its internal experts when the explosion of social media began taking off several years ago.

"We started wondering how do we use these tools to engage with our audience," says MTV's president, Stephen Friedman. "We really had to turn the reins of the entire strategy to our 24- [to] 25-year-old employees who were coordinators of the channels. That made all the difference because they understood that the voice and message on Tumblr has to be a lot different than on Instagram and on Facebook."

Not only did these social media–savvy employees understand the difference among the platforms, but, according to Friedman, they also understood that, fundamentally, the engagement "has to be different than marketing, but based on engaging our audience in a conversation. For much of that message, people are going to be checked out, but if you're giving them something that blurs the line between marketing and content, something that's good information, you're going to do better."

Letting the junior staff lead the charge paid off. The company went from 5 million Facebook fans to more than 100 million within two years. "That means we're reaching as many people on our [TV] screens as we are on Facebook," says Friedman. "That's a profound shift—the letting go of our assumptions about it at the executive level and letting the junior staff lead had a profound impact on why, so far, it's working for us."

How do you make this insight work for your company like it did for MTV? Well, you can simply involve Millennial employees in your digital and social media strategy planning process, just as Elizabeth's employer did.

But you might want to think bigger, Christine Barton, partner at BCG and coauthor of our study, says. "Most companies have a huge millennial population sitting there that is under-tapped in terms of new business ideas for products and marketing. Don't just think about how you can engage them as employees. Think about how you can engage them as consumers of your brands, involving them in your research and development processes and mining them for their insights."

You may also want to consider training them to be brand ambassadors.

"Certainly, there can be egregious abuses of this freedom, so you'll need to institute social media policies," adds Barton. "But in certain categories like apparel and casual dining, allowing your employees to serve as brand advocates can be very advantageous. The millennial consumer wants to interact with people that reflect their values."

Mining this insight, social media marketing company Zuberance, which is focused on converting everyday consumers into brand advocates, has begun to encourage its clients to look inside their own company for these ambassadors. Zuberance has launched an online employee advocacy solution to help them do it.[1]

Through Zuberance's Workforce Advocacy Program, a company is able to identify the best potential advocates for the brand through social media listening tools. Once identified, these brand advocates can provide testimonials for the company and respond to customer feedback, using the Zuberance platform.[2] This is yet another way for a company to put a face on its day-to-day efforts and humanize its image. Such endeavors are likely to be well received by Millennial employees who crave the opportunity to voice their opinions.

At Barkley, Jeff's social media team encourages clients interested in unleashing their young employees' expertise in social media and channeling it in a productive way to embrace the concept of becoming a social business that empowers all constituents, especially employees, to have a voice. The goal is cocreating with their consumers, which can have a positive bottom-line impact.

To get started you'll need an internal "playbook," or strategy, that clearly delineates roles and responsibilities, training efforts, and social media guidelines.

The Mobile Moment of Truth

We'd be remiss if we didn't spend some time looking into the influence of mobile technology on Millennial consumer behavior in this technology-focused chapter.

"When it comes to technology usage, mobile is the most important technology because this generation is primarily connected through their mobile devices," says Mark Logan, senior vice president of Barkley's Innovation Lab, Moonshot, who is currently studying mobile technology and its influence on consumer behavior.

Also easily overlooked is the power of short message service (SMS), a.k.a. texting, over its sexier counterpart, the mobile Web. After all, many Millennials on the lower end of the age range do not have Web-enabled devices. The following case study sheds light on how one nonprofit was able to reengage its target audience—young Millennials—through text.

CASE STUDY: Teen Nonprofit Texts to Reengage and Reconnect with Its Supporters

Who?	Do Something
What?	Do Something, which engages teens in cause campaigns, was having

trouble staying in touch with its target audience members via e-mail, prompting its leadership team to ask: Is there a better way to be in touch?

How? Since taking the helm of the organization in 2003, CEO Nancy Lublin knew Do Something had a digital-first strategy because "that's where teens live these days." After slimming down the organization to just its headquarters in New York City and investing the savings in an interactive website, Lublin made another astute decision: She surrounded herself with smart, young staff members, proudly adding "chief old person" to her title. Not only did these young team members know what marketing messages resonate best with their peers, they also knew what tactics would lead to better and increased engagement, which had long been a challenge for the organization. Texting was the solution.

"About two years ago, the team decided to send out texts to 500 kids they hadn't heard from in six months. I think we'd already sent around 20 emails with no response. These were dead users," says Lublin. "Within nine minutes of sending the text, we had a 20 percent response rate. Everyone was high-fiving each other. A new strategy was born that day."

The organization does most of its campaigns through text, getting teens to opt in to participate. For instance, Do Something's Pregnancy Text campaign, launched in 2012, was created to address the teen pregnancy issue in the United States. The text campaign sent "funny text messages" from a pretend baby throughout the day for a 24-hour period, aiming to show female *and male* teens just how difficult it is to be a young parent. Participants received messages such as "BUURRRPPP. Oops, sorry about the mess on your shirt. It didn't look good on you anyway."

The campaign was a hit, generating more than 100,000 opt-ins. It probably didn't hurt that Do Something also gave away a $2,000 scholarship to one lucky winner, who got five friends to sign up.

Impact?   According to Lublin, not only is text messaging cheap, it generates "killer response rates" for the organization, 15 times higher than for e-mail. The key to success: getting teens to opt in to campaigns they care about and personalizing the message according to their interests.

"Texting is an intimate and more immediate form of communication," says Lublin. "Whenever they see the message, they are able to quickly react. My team is also instructed to quickly respond."

The ultimate goal? Long-term engagement.

"The whole world is talking about mobile, but what they're really talking about is the mobile web. A lot of young people are not yet web enabled. That will likely tip someday, but we remain bullish on text for now," she says. Because we have their local number—something that won't likely change —we are ensured long-term engagement. That's what we care about most."

From our research, we know that Millennials are all about instant gratification, placing a premium on speed, ease, efficiency, and convenience in all of their transactions. Information and answers to their most pressing questions are only a Google search, click, or text away.

"[Young people] have grown up in a world that has come to offer them instant access to nearly the entirety of human knowledge, and incredible opportunities to connect, create, and collaborate," according to Janna Anderson, director of Elon University's Imagining the Internet Center, in an article from TheDigitalShift.com.[3]

Their desire for efficiency in transactions drives many Millennials' purchase decisions these days, whether they're using their smartphones to access user reviews or to compare prices while they're actually in a store. Findings from the recently released "Mobile Moment of Truth" study by Sprint with partners Barkley and Brand Amplitude note that, compared to older Americans, Millennials are more likely to use their smartphones *while* they are shopping, to assist with their purchase decisions. See Figure 3-2.

→ This also applies to conversations of a political nature

'Comparing prices' continues to be a primary use throughout the shopping continuum regardless of age

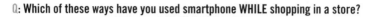

Q: Which of these ways have you used smartphone WHILE shopping in a store?

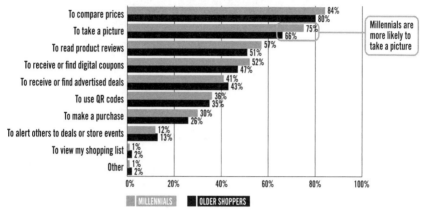

Figure 3-2 Millennials crowdsource while shopping.

Beyond the screens of their smartphones, Millennials' drive toward efficient transactions is displayed in a variety of real-world contexts. Indeed, our research found that Millennials shop for groceries at convenience stores twice as much as non-Millennials. They also value getting through the line quickly in fast casual-format restaurants (81 percent vs. 71 percent) and care less about "friendly" service than "fast" service.

This preference for speed is also reflected in how they participate in causes. Of the Millennials who make direct donations (34 percent), almost half donate via SMS through their mobile devices (15 percent), compared to only 5 percent of non-Millennials. In short, when they know they want something, they want it fast.

But back to mobile technology for a moment—and a Millennial's desire for instant gratification. What does this mean for brands, and why should they even be concerned? For brick-and-mortar retailers, the real fear here is that retailers may fall victim to the "showroom" effect—in essence becoming Amazon's showroom—as John Jannarone warned in a WSJ.com article:

> It has become much easier for consumers to compare prices—ironically, using applications on the smartphones they can purchase in Best Buy. Shoppers can visit Best Buy stores to examine items before buying them elsewhere.[4]

Millennials view the retail stores as places where they can see, touch, and try on a potential purchase. It is not necessarily the place where they will make the purchase because they want to price-comparison shop first. According to the Sprint "Mobile Moment of Truth" study, an overwhelming number of Millennial shoppers—84 percent—use their smartphones and price-comparison apps to compare prices while shopping.

Because Millennials are conducting price comparisons while in stores, leading them to buy products elsewhere, it's no surprise that Best Buy and other brick-and-mortar stores' stock prices have taken a hit lately. Can Best Buy and other retailers that have lost market share to companies like Amazon bounce back? It's all about winning what Mark Logan refers to as the "mobile moment of truth."

"There's a growing amount of data out that points to Millennials using their mobile devices while shopping in-aisle, but what's not clearly known with any detail is what tools, apps and sites they are using, and how that shapes purchase decisions," Logan says. "What makes a Millennial decide to purchase that something in-store versus buying on Amazon, often at a discount, versus not buying it at all? It's this mobile moment of truth that retailers have to first gain intelligence on and then address. This is why a retailer's mobile website is likely more important than their website now."

First step? Retailers need to recognize they are starting at an advantage because customers have already chosen to walk into their stores, Logan says. Capitalize on that advantage by channeling them to your preferred mobile platform, where you satisfy their desire to get product reviews by providing product reviews from your own community.

"You would prefer that they didn't use Amazon's price checking app while they're in your store," says Logan. "Data shows that shoppers who use your native apps or website are far more likely to convert in store. Give them QR codes or mobile URLs or other visual cues that direct them to your mobile sites and apps."

Good advice. But taking a step back, retailers won't arrive at that mobile moment of truth if customers aren't even stepping into their stores. What do you do about that? According to Ted Hurlbut, principal of retail and management consultants Hurlbut & Associates, in addition to selling products and services that consumers want or need, retailers must also find ways "to re-engage customers on more than just a rational level, to make shopping in their stores a more stimulating and satisfying experience, rather than just another trip to pick up whatever is on sale."[5]

Our research found that Millennials want integrated online and offline shopping experiences. In order to get Millennials to keep coming into stores and spending money, the new mall "purchase pathway" model must combine "live price-comparison research with the mobile, social, and online interactions that this generation craves," such as the ability to discuss experiences and share recommendations with friends, according to an article that Jeff coauthored with our research partners at BCG.[6]

Retailers can also look to tap popular apps like Shopkick, which offers customers rewards and points for entering a store and making a purchase, and allow for the use of digital wallets, which permit shoppers to pay with their mobile devices, to win over members of this on-the-go generation.

Offline, Millennials say they want stores to provide for easy or discounted delivery, and they want the option of going to a brick-and-mortar store to pick up or return their online purchases.

Mark Logan adds that "magical and novel in-store experiences" through the use of technology and mobile can also play an important role in getting Millennials to shop and spend money with retailers.

"The digital and physical worlds are no longer separate realms. Technology has the ability to facilitate and enhance real world experiences in ways that are novel, surprising and delightful," Logan explains.

Examples of this can be found in the number of new augmented-reality technologies that are popping up and shaping the Millennial shopping experience. Consider Monocle, which combines the global-positioning-system and camera features on a user's phone to help diners find the best eateries in the area via Yelp reviews. Or Google's emerging Project Glass, a device that will let users project a variety of applications on the world around them by wearing special, computerized glasses.

In the retail space, Nike opened a store—Nike+ FuelStation & NIKEiD Studio—in East London during the 2012 Olympics that pretty much "raise[d] the bar on what experiential digital looks like for brands and consumers," according to one blog on the store's launch.[7]

Located in the world's first pop-up mall, a temporary shopping center made out of shipping containers, the store employed engaging digital experiences that aimed to empower runners. Examples of such include augmented reality displays, LED walls, and digital mannequins.

Pretty cool, right? Apple is another company that wins points among Millennials for its magical in-store experiences, which keep these consumers coming in by the droves.

"The sense of wonder and discovery that I get every time I walk into an Apple store is amazing. I am always learning or seeing something new and have an enjoyable brand experience when I interact with them," said one Millennial consumer in response to our survey.

In a *Harvard Business Review* article, Ron Johnson, former vice president of retail for Apple, explains how the Apple example dispels the idea that brick-and-mortar stores are irrecoverably broken:

> Look at the Apple Stores, which have annual sales averaging $40 million per store in a category that in 2000 everyone said would move entirely to the Internet. Today the Apple Stores are the highest-performing stores in the history of retailing. Physical stores are still the primary way people acquire merchandise, and I think that will be true 50 years from now.[8]

Indeed, walk by any Apple store today and the notion of brick-and-mortar stores losing traffic to online retailers gets quickly tossed aside.

"Novelty and delight are motivators for sharing an experience that excites you, and you're far more likely to want to share it with friends," says Mark Logan. "Technology can be a critical component in elevating something from 'That's kind of cool' to

'Wow, I need to share this.' Nike certainly had that 'wow' factor in their [London] store."

In addition to this seamless integration of technology into the brand experience, companies need to be willing to reexamine or rethink their existing customer service models to meet the needs of these on-the-go consumers.

As you'll see in the following case study, Nike and Apple are not alone. Sephora is making its transaction process more efficient, setting the bar for the beauty industry.

CASE STUDY: Beauty Retailer Gets a "Social Business" Makeover

Who?   Sephora

What?   Sephora, a long-time retail leader in the digital space being one of the first beauty retail brands to have a Web presence in the late 1990s, is aiming to stay ahead of the curve with a "social business"–driven strategy.

Driven by advances in social and mobile technology, e-commerce has been radically transformed, according to Sephora senior vice president and digital head Julie Bornstein, explaining the reasoning behind the push toward digital integration.[9]

The changes, which feature a new personalized Web experience, new mobile site, and iPhone app, are aimed to attract the next generation of consumers while providing current customers a superior shopping experience.

"We're giving people a great experience today, and we're also keeping up with the new generation of shoppers. My kids don't know life without an iPad. We're making sure that Gen Y, Millennials, Gen Z are able to shop the way they expect to," Bornstein explains.

How? In the summer of 2011, the company began testing iPads at 20 stores around the country as a way to let customers navigate Sephora's thousands of products and get access to makeup and hairstyling tips. In addition to the pilot, every Sephora store is now outfitted with iPod Touches, enabling mobile points of sale that allow busy young consumers to purchase right on the spot. Shoppers also get instant access to their purchase history or rewards program points. "No lines, no hassle," Bornstein says.

Impact? While the direct impact of these changes on the bottom line is yet unknown, Sephora is already winning rave reviews, nabbing the top spot on L2's Prestige 100® Mobile IQ report in 2012. Developed in partnership with New York University Stern School of Business professor Scott Galloway, the ranking measures the mobile competence of 100 iconic brands across five industries—Beauty & Skincare, Fashion, Hospitality, Retail, and Watches & Jewelry—using 250 data points across four dimensions (Mobile Sites, Mobile Apps, Mobile Marketing, and Innovation & Integration).

The bottom line for brands when it comes to the mobile moment of truth?

"For Millennials, technology is not a thing unto itself. It is just part of the environment, like furniture," says Mark Logan. "Brands need to find that right balance between technology and treating it like it's no big deal but integrating and leveraging the hell out of it. That's the art—making it a big deal internally, but pretending it's not externally."

Look at all mobile dimensions of your brand. How does the mobile device facilitate or enhance the in-store experience? How might it play into a loyalty program? Is this the gateway to mapping purchasing behavior? It's not about having a mobile marketing strategy but a mobile *brand* strategy.

Never forget the ultimate goal of these efforts: to get Millennials to spend more time with your brand. If you can achieve that, you've struck gold.

CHAPTER 3: KEY TAKEAWAYS

▸ **Millennials are early adopters of technology.** Millennials are 2.5 times more likely to try out the latest technology. If you ask them the all-important question of whether or not to upgrade, more often than not, they will choose to upgrade. Brands should seize this opportunity to gain Millennial loyalty from the start.

▸ **Millennials are serving as the household CTO,** indirectly influencing household purchase decisions to the tune of $500 billion each year. Invest in understanding how Millennials are carrying and translating your brand message to adults and be willing to help these conversations along.

▸ **Millennials feel they should be rewarded for being smart and doing things well in the workplace.** Tap your employees' eagerness to provide crucial insights into your products and services and reward them accordingly.

▸ **Millennials are more likely to "showroom" while shopping,** using price-comparison apps while in-store to find better deals. Develop a mobile brand strategy to get Millennials to spend more time with your brand and ultimately win the "mobile moment of truth."

▸ **Millennials must first be engaged.** None of the preceding points mentioned that takeaways can be achieved without first securing Millennial engagement. Make your brand experience more stimulating and satisfying, and gain Millennial attention.

created a profile on a social networking site, and 80 percent sleep with their cell phones next to them.[2]

A University of Michigan Social Research study found that 80 to 90 percent of Millennials use social media, three out of four have created a profile on a social networking site, and 80 percent sleep with their cell phones next to them.

Is this "always on" characteristic just a Millennial thing? It turns out that Millennials and non-Millennials actually spend about the same amount of time per week online, about 11 to 20 hours, not including e-mail handling. They also go online for some of the same things, including shopping, weather updates, news updates, and navigation directions.

However, *it's what they do with that time that makes the difference.* As you might guess from the number of entertainment-based devices they own, Millennials spend a lot of their time seeking entertainment online, including playing games, watching streaming TV, listening to music, and reading Web magazines.

Time-shifting technologies and sites such as Netflix and Hulu.com have completely transformed the way people view television and movies, and Millennials are at the forefront of this trend. In fact, the Millennial generation's TV viewing habits are causing a lot of concern among the major media companies these days. Let's start with the research. While Millennials still watch live television, our study found they watch it much less often than non-Millennials, and they watch it on their own terms.

"I've never had cable TV, because of the cost. And really there is no reason to have it," says Peter L., age 24. "I'm only really interested in specific shows on TV, and will watch it at a friend's or go online to see ones I really want to see. *The Daily Show*

Build a Listening and Participation Strateg

If there is a brand I really like, I want to help them and
would even be willing to take an online survey for free c
even participate in a focus group, if I had time to help th
out. If there is a brand I hate, I want to tell them why.
—*Megan L., 27, Philadelphia, Pennsyl*

Millennials are "always on," as we noted in Chapter
access to multiple Web-enabled devices, at home and o
makes them power users of the Internet, who, like M
willing to engage with and help not only their favorite bi
those that they don't like. In some cases, they are even v
serve as brand advocates.

According to a Center for Media Research brief, the
nial generation "is unique from other generations in that
the first generation to be always connected,"[1] a finding b
a University of Michigan Social Research study that fou
90 percent of Millennials use social media, three out of

[with Jon Stewart] and *The Colbert Report. Parks and Recreation,* another favorite, is also available online."

Peter is not alone, as you can see in Figure 4-1, Millennials watch less TV overall and prefer to watch it *when they want to watch it.*

MILLENNIALS AND TV

They watch less and watch it on their terms

Source: Barkley, The Boston Consulting Group, and Service Management Group, "American Millennials: Deciphering the Enigma Generation," September 2011.

Figure 4-1 An overview of Millennial TV consumption.

Why this difference in TV viewing habits? For starters, price. For a cash-strapped Millennial, the average cable subscription fee, typically $75 a month or even more if you want access to premium channels like HBO, according to CNNMoney.com,[3] is hard to swallow. This is especially true when the package includes hundreds of channels with little or no appeal. Also, this is a generation accustomed to having it their way thanks to the Internet, which has made a lot of content available free of charge. Furthermore, companies like Apple have popularized the à la carte approach through its iTunes platform. When you have so many entertainment options to choose from, the TV set is no longer the necessity it used to be. So, many Millennials are cutting the cable.

An article in *The Atlantic* referred to Millennials as "the cheapest generation,"[4] when it comes to their consumer habits. We think this is more a sign of consumer savvy. They are willing to spend money on things they care about, but they value things differently than older generations. We'll dive deeper into this issue later in the book.

In terms of additional online usage, Millennials tend to subscribe to Web and news feeds in greater numbers, and thanks to social media platforms like Twitter, Millennials are able to pick and choose, customizing the type of information they receive and when they receive it.

But where it gets really interesting is in the time Millennials spend *producing* and *uploading online content,* including photos, videos, wiki entries, blog posts, microblog posts, and product and service reviews. For every piece of content that gets produced, there exists an online platform—Facebook, Twitter, Instagram, Yelp, YouTube, Tumblr, or Foursquare—where their opinions can be broadcast to a wider audience. With the number of news and talk-show programs that give on-air time to these opinions shared via a Tweet or Facebook update, a Millennial's power to influence others is boundless.

According to a March 2011 report from Forrester Research,[5] nearly three-quarters of 12- to 17-year olds (74 percent) use social networks to talk about products with friends and make recommendations. Although the report concerned a slightly younger age range, our research backs this up. As we noted in Chapter 1, 60 percent of Millennials participate in this activity, compared to 29 percent of non-Millennials.

Rudy Wilson, the former Frito-Lay marketing executive introduced earlier, explains: "[This] generation is empowered thanks to these digital and social tools they are extremely adept at using. They know they can make an impact on things and are trying to act on it."

Not only are they more active online, but many Millennials *want* brands to engage with them online and through social media.

But this doesn't mean that brands need to be bombarding Millennial consumers on Facebook. According to the same Forrester report, not all young people want to be friends with brands. Indeed, only 6 percent of 12- to 17-year-olds who use the Web want to be friends with a brand on Facebook.[6]

> *Not only are Millennials more active online, but they want brands to engage with them online and through social media. But this doesn't mean that brands should bombard Millennial consumers on Facebook. Not all young people want to be friends with brands.*

"Many brands are looking to social media as a strong digital channel to communicate with these consumers, since it's where [they] are spending so much time," wrote Jacqueline Anderson, Forrester's former consumer insights analyst and author of the report. "But research shows that it is important to consider more than just consumers' propensity to use a specific channel. Almost half of 12- to 17-year-olds don't think brands should have a presence using social tools at all."

So where does this leave us? These findings call for a "listening" strategy—a more nuanced approach to engaging with Millennials online. This approach will become increasingly important as the generation following the Millennials grows up. According to the same Forrester report, "[Brands] might be better off being more reactive than proactive, and they should listen."[7] Indeed, the study found that just 16 percent of young consumers expect brands to use social media to interact with them, and 28 percent expect those brands to listen to what they say on social sites and get back to them. However, it's worth noting that this report is from 2011 and these percentages of those who expect a response from brands have likely increased.

"[W]hen [brands] are specifically invited into the conversation (in this case by calling out the brand), they are ready to join in and add something meaningful to the conversation," says Anderson in an *AdWeek* article about the report. "But, they should blend into the background otherwise."[8]

We couldn't agree more. This brings us back to the Ford Fiesta tale we shared in Chapter 1. What made Ford's interaction with Janelle such a success was how they *listened* to and *responded* to her needs. By focusing their interaction with her on meeting her specific needs—helping her get the car she wanted and *letting her do the promotion*—they gained better brand awareness among many more Millennials. As we pointed out earlier, the nonintrusive and authentic way they interacted with Janelle won a brand advocate for life.

Morton's The Steakhouse is another example of a brand that seized an opportunity to listen to its consumers and create a loyal advocate for life. Back in 2011, businessman Peter Shankman was boarding an airplane after a long day of meetings. He'd be landing at Newark Airport just in time for dinner, and a juicy Morton's steak seemed like the perfect solution to the growing hunger in his belly. With little more than a passing thought, Shankman jokingly tweeted at Morton's, requesting that the restaurant deliver a porterhouse steak to him upon his arrival. Sure enough, when he got off the plane, much to his surprise, Shankman was greeted by a Morton's employee with a steak, including all the fixin's! Shankman promptly took to Twitter to express how impressed he was with the brand. The story was picked up by major media outlets, including *The Huffington Post*,[9] generating even more brand awareness and goodwill for Morton's far beyond this one very satisfied customer.

Now, two interesting things to note with this story: Not only is Shankman a well-known social media guru with quite a following online, but he was a dedicated Morton's brand advocate long before this incident. But that's not the main point here. Because Morton's went the extra mile for him, Shankman was also willing to go the extra mile in spreading the news of this incredible gesture of goodwill.

The Participation Economy

"The opportunity to participate in a company's product and service offering—it's not an ask but an expectation from the [Millennial] generation," says Rudy Wilson, the former Frito-Lay vice president you met earlier.

Because of this expectation, many companies and brands (as in the previous Ford example) are testing the social engagement waters, giving young consumers a voice and an opportunity to participate in the product and service offering.

The problem is, companies tend to do it as a one-off rather than focusing on the opportunity to build a lasting relationship—the real advantage that the participation economy enables.

"Marketing is all about building a relationship, but a lot of brands today are doing one-offs, taking a one-night stand approach to relationships," explains Wilson. "But Millennials are savvy. They are willing to invest in you as much as you invest in them. Brands that approach the relationship with these young consumers as a lifetime one versus a one-night stand will enjoy higher returns."

Our participation economy model, first mentioned in Chapter 1, sheds light on how companies can move beyond those one-night stands toward lifetime relationships. The ultimate goal: the creation of a group of eager young brand advocates.

"The most important question for every brand today is to figure out how to turn those people who are just 'meh' about the product or service into brand advocates—people who love you, fight for you, answer people's questions on the brand's behalf, etc.," says Joe Cox, Jeff's colleague and Barkley's social media director. "Of course, you have to start with a product or service that is worth fighting for. It has to be something worthy of advocacy. Brands should start there and then build a strategy around it that engages the community it naturally attracts."

So let's first assume you have that advocacy-worthy product or service. Next? You have to figure out who is already talking about your brand.

"Find out where those conversations are happening and who your advocates already are, because if you're selling a product, there are people who are already talking about it online," says Cox. "Social media monitoring tools like Radian6 or Spiral16 and others can help find and identify who these people are."

Why start here? To grow, engage, and activate a group of advocates, you must first build a base. It sounds like campaigning for public office, right? Well, you kind of are.

"Think about how [President] Obama won in 2008. He first built a base of supporters largely using popular social media tools like Facebook, and when the time was right, he leveraged the heck out of it to win," says Cox. "Building a community is like tending a garden. It's a lot of work up front and you have to be patient before it begins to bear fruit. Advocates are like Miracle-Gro, which ensures a healthy crop."

The "Right" Strategy

In the past, brand marketing was a one-way street where brand managers controlled the entire process. Over the past decade, the process has evolved to allow two-way conversations between brands and consumers, thanks in large part to advances in technology and social media. Some would argue it's even more than a two-way street.

"It's a web of consumers talking to brands, talking to other consumers and so forth," Jacqueline Anderson says.

Bottom line: If your brand isn't taking advantage of the opportunity to have a conversation with consumers that's easily facilitated through social media, you're missing a huge opportunity.

"[Millennials] want that constant engagement. It's that participatory sense of 'I'm in it with you,'" says MTV's Stephen Friedman. "It's fascinating, but our audience wants their favorite music artist to engage with them through Twitter or Facebook, and they want to reward them by buying the album. They still know where to get it free but they feel more invested and protective of the artist if they've got that more personal connection."

The same goes for brands. The more they invest in engaging with consumers the right way, the bigger the payoff will be in terms of increased goodwill, better online engagement, *and* higher sales figures. Pepsi is a great example.

Like most brands, Pepsi is active on the relevant social media platforms like Facebook, Twitter, and YouTube. However, unlike a lot of brands, Pepsi has completely changed the way it markets to Millennial consumers with its most recent, Millennial-targeted "Live For Now" campaign.

The new Pepsi experience instantly begins when you visit the website www.pepsi.com. The "digital dashboard" or Pepsi's home page displays numerous tweets and conversations taking place with its consumers. Immediately, you see how important its consumers' opinions are to Pepsi. In fact, for a 2012 Pepsi concert series featuring major artists, the dashboard and tweets from the live audience and people watching it online were used to determine the song selection and encores.

"[I]f you want to remain relevant with this new type of consumer, you have to be where they are, you have to talk their language, and you have to connect with them in a way that keeps them feeling like they want to be part of your brand," says Brian Solis, a principal analyst at the Altimeter Group and author of "What's the Future of Business," as quoted in a *U.S. News & World Report* article.[10]

The Pepsi transformation is gaining speed with Millennials. Pepsi is using the content created and curated by its own consumers both to help push the brand forward by creating more conversations and maintaining relevance and to keep up to date with its consumers by tracking what they're saying.

Pepsi also realized that this social media–driven strategy can help it learn more about its consumers because it allows for better tracking of visits, mentions, and likes and the quick identification of disgruntled customers it can direct to its customer service department before things get out of hand. Similarly, Pepsi uses location-based marketing to better tailor content to different demographics.

What impact have these efforts had? With more than 1 million Twitter followers, more than 9 million likes on Facebook, and more than 50 million YouTube video views, Pepsi shows that a smart social media strategy—one that draws on the tenets of the participation economy model we'll detail in the next section—pays off with consumers, especially members of this generation.

Let's spend some time fleshing out each aspect of the participation economy and how it plays out in today's brand marketing process.

Engagement (New) vs. Interruption (Old)

As you learned in previous chapters, Millennials desire a higher degree of engagement. What better way to get to know these consumers than to engage with them, says Brand Amplitude's Carol Phillips. "Rather than create messages, strive for cultural as well as brand relevance."

One surefire way to achieve cultural relevance is by continuously providing engaging content—information that's valuable to this generation. In industry parlance, this is called "content marketing" (with less emphasis on "marketing," as Millennials hate to feel like they're being marketed to). It's become a hot topic for brands looking for better ways to engage their target consumers.

What makes content engaging or—more simply—great? According to Joe Pulizzi, a leading content marketing thinker and founder of the Content Marketing Institute: "There are all kinds of definitions of great content. However, if we think about it from an engagement standpoint, great content is information that makes people take an action. In the social media context, we like to think about great content that people are willing to share with their networks through outlets like Twitter, Facebook or other social communities. If, as a business, you develop content that is good enough for people to share with those that matter most to them, you've created great content."[11]

In definition form, according to Pulizzi, content marketing consists of "creating and distributing relevant and valuable content to attract, acquire and engage a clearly defined and understood target audience, with the objective of driving profitable customer action."[12]

It's the kind of content that can turn a mere customer into a brand advocate. And it makes sense. Consumers today say they trust editorial or earned media placements more than advertisements, according to a 2012 Nielsen report.[13] We do; don't you?

As a telltale sign of its significance, Facebook has tipped its hat to engagement, going so far as to reward and promote companies and brands for providing engaging content. Through their EdgeRank algorithm, content that generates the most engagement through "likes," comments, and shares is automatically identified and promoted by the social media site to the top of the News Feed, guaranteeing an even greater amount of exposure.

According to Joe Cox, "In the past, consumers had no choice but to be passive participants in media, just letting broadcasts wash over them, not offering consumers the opportunity to say that something was completely useless or untruthful. Social media has fundamentally changed that by giving them a voice in the form of a 'like' or a re-tweet."

For a real-world example, check out how Coca-Cola uses a content marketing strategy to engage consumers, winning rave reviews from brand marketing experts.

CASE STUDY: Brand Puts All Its Eggs in "Content Marketing" Basket

Who?   Coca-Cola

What?   Coca-Cola has developed its
                    Content 2020 strategy to ensure
                    the 100-year-old brand remains
                    relevant to target consumers, who
                    increasingly demand more valuable
                    content from the companies they
                    support.

Coca-Cola's Jonathan Mildenhall, vice president for global advertising strategy and creative excellence and visionary behind the strategy, explains the philosophy behind Content 2020 in an interview: "All advertisers need a lot more content so that they can keep the engagement with consumers fresh and relevant, because of the 24/7 connectivity. If you're going to be successful around the world, you have to have fat and fertile ideas at the core."[14]

How?   According to the Content 2020
                    manifesto video posted to YouTube
                    by the company, "Coca-Cola must
                    create the world's most compelling
                    content, [and] can no longer rely on
                    being 30-Second-TV-Centric."[15]

Well, how do they do that? Through "brand stories so contagious they can't be controlled (i.e., they're liquid) and are innately relevant to business objectives, brand, and consumer interests (i.e., they're linked)," according to a Content Marketing Institute blog post.[16]

Now, not all content will be "contagious." Some will simply be about keeping a dialogue going with brand advocates during the lulls when there's no compelling story to share.

The Content 2020 strategy deploys a mix of content offerings for consumers to fill those lulls, with content falling into one of three categories:

- 70 percent will be low-risk, bread-and-butter content that supports the overarching theme but can be developed fairly quickly, for example, responding to consumer questions via Twitter or asking fans questions on Facebook. It's the daily conversation you'd have while passing your colleagues in the hallway at work, for instance.

- 20 percent will be an expansion of the bread-and-butter content that works.

- 10 percent will revolve around completely new ideas that likely involve high production costs such as the creation of video.

Also, the company "is well aware of the deluge of content, and will aim for ruthless editing so it doesn't just add to all the noise out there. In other words, Coca-Cola recognizes that it needs to continually re-imagine, not just replicate, its content," according to the Content Marketing Institute.[17]

Impact?   While it's still too soon to tell what impact the Content 2020 strategy will have on Coke's quest to build more engaged brand advocates, there are some early signs of success.

Throughout 2010 and 2011, Coke "punk'd" a bunch of college students on campuses throughout the country with its "Happiness Vending Machine," which spontaneously dispensed surprises to unsuspecting students. The students' reactions—of course, priceless and captured on hidden camera by the company—instantly went viral on the Web. This relatively simple idea of dispensing surprises was a huge public relations coup for the company. No amount of expensive paid advertising could have had the same impact as this compelling video.

To sum up the Coca-Cola case study and its content-driven "engagement" strategy: "[Coca-Cola] knows that through good and valuable content, they are more likely to be a part of someone's life," Cox says of the company's content-first efforts.

Taking a humorous and story-driven approach to selling men's deodorant, Old Spice has managed to distinguish itself from the competition by showcasing a comical brand advocate in hilarious commercials that become instant Internet sensations.

If you take a look at Old Spice's social media platforms, you can see the brand isn't messing around when it comes to staying relevant and reaching its target consumers. The Old Spice Facebook page—regularly updated with funny comments, videos, and pictures—has reached more than 2 million likes. Its other social media platforms have accomplished similar feats with more than 15,000 followers on Instagram, more than 223,000 on Twitter, and 300 million-plus video views on YouTube. Clearly, the brand has made an impact.

Likewise, in a recently released YouTube video, Old Spice let fans in on the filming of the latest commercial with its most well-known brand advocate, Isaiah Mustafa.[18] This created yet another opportunity for Old Spice to engage with consumers—many of whom are Millennials seeking brands that provide a unique experience.

So just exactly why has Old Spice's reinvented approach to marketing been so popular with Millennials? Simply put, the brand has created a story that Millennials are interested in reading. It has put an engaging and entertaining face to the brand. Now Old Spice can talk more about the brand without focusing solely on the product.

Interaction (New) vs. Reaction (Old)

Next on our participation economy agenda is the difference between *reaction* (the old way) and *interaction* (the new way) when it comes to a brand marketing strategy.

Really, it's a matter of simply building on the foundation of engagement, which we covered in the previous section. Why wouldn't you, as a brand, want to continue interacting with those engaged and eager brand advocates you've already begun to build? You wouldn't.

In the past, without these instantaneous feedback channels, brands had no opportunity for the interaction they can have today. But now? Well, there's no excuse not to.

This point gets back to that expectation that Rudy Wilson talked about earlier in the chapter: Millennial consumers expect brands to interact with them when things go right—and wrong. Do you remember that United Airlines public relations snafu several years ago that featured damning headlines such as "United Airlines Breaks Guitars"? If not, here's a recap: Canadian musician Dave Carroll's favorite Taylor guitar did not fare well on a United Air trip, arriving in the baggage claim essentially destroyed. The culprit? He and his fellow passengers had witnessed the airline's baggage-handling crew throwing guitars on the tarmac. Despite the fact that Carroll witnessed the mishandling himself, the airline refused to compensate him for the damage after multiple requests via e-mail, leaving the musician no alternative but to air his grievances in a song that he posted to YouTube. Long story short, the video and song went viral, hitting number one on the iTunes music store a week after its release, finally forcing the company to relent and compensate Carroll. But it was too late; the damage to the brand's image was done. Had United Air simply interacted with the disgruntled traveler, paying him for the damage for which it was responsible, the company would have avoided the public backlash.

In addition to being ready to interact with consumers when things go wrong, brands also need to be proactive in interacting when things go right. Take *The Hunger Games* book series and movie, which was a huge cultural phenomenon. Rather than resting on their laurels (and spending the big checks that had arrived by the truckload on their doorsteps), the creators made a smart move in launching a *Hunger Games* game on Facebook, helping them build on the momentum with brand advocates who were "hungry" for more.

"Fans were looking for new ways to interact with and engage with the brand after the movie," Joe Cox explains. "And the game fulfilled this desire. It was a smart move, as it allowed the creators to keep their fan base engaged until the next movie comes out."

With one-off campaigns, brands enjoy a giant spike in interest from consumers, but then they lose them. By using interactive tactics, you keep your brand advocates engaged until the next big launch.

This realization inspired MTV's content strategy with the popular *Teen Wolf* series, which you'll learn more about in the following case study.

CASE STUDY: TV Show Manages to Grow Its Audience and Popularity Even While Off-Air

Who:	MTV
What:	In 2012, *Teen Wolf* had just launched its second season on MTV. Despite having been on the eight-month hiatus that most scripted shows take to film the next season, the popular show had been steadily growing its fan base during the break. How? MTV invested in a "bridge strategy," partnering with Jeff Davis, the show's creator, on a nine-month-long narrative that was carried out

with fans on several social media platforms.

"The nice thing about working with these young creators of shows like *Teen Wolf* is they understand the importance of engaging with their fans, want to play in that space and don't want to let go of that audience," MTV president Stephen Friedman says of the strategy.

How: Through tweets, Facebook messages, Tumblr blog posts, and online videos, MTV created a multi-month online campaign dedicated to *Teen Wolf* that had fans working to solve a mystery through online interactions with the show's creator and cast members. To top it off, MTV launched a contest that rewarded one community member with a trip to the set as they were shooting the second season.

"There was a hunger from the audience, who didn't want it to end last season," says Friedman. "We all experience that same feeling that you can't wait for a show that you love to come back, but . . . we realized that, with [the Millennial] generation, the online fervor was still there."

Impact? By the end of the "bridge," *Teen Wolf* had increased its fan base on Facebook by 50 percent, and when the second season launched, it enjoyed a 26 percent bump up in ratings from the year before.

"This could not have happened if the audience had not demanded it," says Friedman. "Certainly, some of the fans will never want to engage online, and prefer to just watch the show. This strategy allowed us to create multiple layers to a season, leading to a much tighter relationship between audience and shows, which is always appealing to sponsors."

Before moving on, let's home in on one aspect of MTV's strategy: the use of virtual communities.

In addition to allowing brands to generate a more passionate fan base, online communities are also good for research and surveying purposes.

Carol Phillips has had much success with her own 200+-member Millennial Super Consumer Community, in which users are tapped for insights into client-sponsored surveys in exchange for gift cards.

If you're considering the launch of your own market research online community (MROC), do be aware that, like raising a puppy, it takes time and money, and the payoff isn't likely to be immediate, as Joe Cox explains: "Most chief marketing officers have the most trouble with this because they are getting pressure on prioritizing what happens in this quarter, and unlike some advertising strategies, can't do it by just throwing money at it. Engaged, healthy and profitable communities don't happen in a quarter. You have to put resources, into growing and shepherding a community. Only after you've done this, do you get the fruit that is ROI."

Jacqueline Anderson also cautions that there needs to be a balance—a give-and-take—when using MROCs.

"The most successful communities occur when the members feel like they are being heard, and are also getting information back," says Anderson. "You will have key members in the community who are providing the most useful insights on product and marketing ideas. But you need to then reward them for their contributions like sharing upcoming releases beforehand. Otherwise, what's in it for them?"

Need an example? *People StyleWatch* has found great success in tapping consumer insight on behalf of advertising partners through its Style Hunters campaign, which "leverages digital ambassadors—1,000 StyleWatch loyalists culled from an A-list panel of 13,000 readers—that receive access to exclusive content and product offers from brands and then disseminate them to their own networks of fashion-forward friends and acquaintances," as detailed in a FolioMag.com article.[19]

Here's how it works, according to the article: "Campaign advertisers float special offers and other exclusive content (product samples, event invitations, special discounts, video) to the *People StyleWatch* team, who then pass it on to their 1,000 Style Hunters. From there, some of the content is blogged about and much of it is passed on virally through Facebook, Twitter and email."[20]

Just as Anderson suggested, Style Hunters is a success because it taps the most influential readers with the strongest social ties online. These readers are deeply engaged thanks to the special perks they receive from advertising partners. For the advertiser, it's an effective way to reach organic or new customers, according to FolioMag.com, due to "the combination of a robust influencer group, especially in fashion, and the viral nature of social media."[21]

So just how successful was this program? According to *People StyleWatch*, it has generated more than 35 million overall impressions for its partner brands.[22]

Engaged Participants (New) vs. Heavy Users (Old)

In the past, brands were aware that there were differences among members of their customer bases—some were heavy users and many weren't, for instance. The challenge (often impossible) was to figure out what caused someone to become a heavy user and whether the same trigger(s) could be used to turn the casual consumer into a heavy user as well.

"It's the 80/20 rule," explains Joe Cox. "Twenty percent of the consumer base (the heavy user) is typically responsible for 80 percent of the profits, so obviously brands want more on those heavy users. It just wasn't so obvious what made a heavy user in the past."

Today, real-time channels such as the online communities help brands get a better sense of what causes someone to become a heavy user—knowledge that can turn more consumers into heavy *and* engaged participants in the shortest amount of time.

Starbucks has also been testing the use of virtual communities with its most loyal customers. Through its MyStarbucks Idea.com platform, customers can log in, submit their ideas for the brand, and even rate other customer ideas.[23] And they're not just seeking new product ideas. Customers are asked to tip off the company about in-store experience and community service-focused involvement ideas, as well. In exchange for their time and input, participants are awarded points for sharing their ideas, receiving positive posts about their ideas, or commenting on or voting for someone else's ideas. The top 10 point collectors are recognized on the site's leaderboard each month.

What makes this different from other online communities or those suggestion boxes of yesteryear? The sheer number of people who actively participate in this venture and the company's commitment to putting the best ideas into action. Indeed, there have been more than 94,000 new product ideas, 31,000 experience ideas, and 20,000 involvement ideas posted. There is also a section on the site called "Ideas In Action," where participants can track their own ideas and see which are being reviewed, which are coming soon, and which have been officially launched. And Starbucks is launching many of these members' ideas. That free beverage you get on your birthday when you sign up as a member of the program? You can thank customer suggestions on MyStarbucksIdea.com for that freebie. This is a great example of a brand that is not only listening to its consumers but willing to take the extra significant step of executing their ideas.

Another company that was frequently named a favorite by the Millennials interviewed for this book is Chipotle. The reason often revolves around how Chipotle engages its biggest fans (those heavy users) in its marketing tactics.

"I love Chipotle's marketing because it's all fun stuff like their Boorito day on Halloween—if you dress up like a farm animal you get a free burrito," says Caroline. "Of course I participated and again on Valentine's Day when you can get a free one for kissing someone!"

The fun, carried out by in-the-know and engaged consumers like Caroline, is spread to other consumers, who quickly become caught up in the excitement.

Personal Gestures (New) vs. Big Promises (Old)

Long gone are the days when a brand could make infomercial-style promises without the goods to back it up.

"Social backchannels have become instant bullshit meters," says Joe Cox. "And brands that can't master transparent communication will experience the wrath of the connected consumer."

No one wants to be treated as a number, especially Millennials.

"Millennials detest stereotypes and won't bother to engage with your brand if they think you're over-generalizing your message," says Carol Phillips. "Unfortunately, the reality is it's not cost effective to market to one."

However, while Millennials expect certain things from brands in terms of participation and engagement, they aren't necessarily expecting a brand to personally reach out to them, which is why the "personal gesture" tactic should be added to every brand's playbook. As you learned in Chapter 1 through Janelle's interaction with Ford, the simple act of tweeting information back or addressing customer service issues upon learning of problems can lead to big public relation wins for brands.

"When Coke retweets your tweet, you're going to be jazzed. You think, 'This brand is not only listening to me, but they're talking to me directly!'" says Cox. "Through social media, brands for [the] first time ever can reach out and say, 'Joe Normal, you rock.' By doing simple things that hold social equity, brands will win over Millennial consumers not yet expecting that personal touch."

A great example of a personal gesture from a brand comes from KLM Royal Dutch Airlines. The story begins with a Dutch filmmaker tweeting at KLM Airlines about the need to have more direct flights from Amsterdam to Miami. At the time, a large music festival was taking place in Miami during spring break, and the first available flight from Amsterdam to Miami would cause all of the Amsterdam-based DJs and producers to miss the festivities. After the filmmaker tweeted at KLM, the airline responded with a challenge: Get a group together by December 6 to fill the flight, and KLM will schedule it. Well, the challenge was accepted, and soon a website and a "Fly2Miami" Twitter account were launched to promote the effort. Within a few hours of grassroots promotion by the filmmaker and fellow supporters, the flight was fully booked, flabbergasting the company, which promptly scheduled the flight.[24]

This is an excellent example of a brand valuing the needs of its customers and delivering what the consumers ask for. Had KLM not been present on Twitter, actively listening to its customers, it would have missed a fantastic opportunity.

Do realize, however, that once situations like the KLM example become the standard, such one-on-one interactions will become an expectation among consumers. Cox maintains that brands have about three more years of opportunity with this tactic.

It's also the company's responsibility to ensure that the message is carried out in every interaction with the Millennial consumers, whether through the company blog or through social media interaction.

Says Jacqueline Anderson, "Certainly, it takes money to make this assessment of how consumers envision the brand, find out the gaps and fix that message. But this solid foundation of understanding and applying throughout the organization is especially important when reaching out to Millennials through social media. Companies need to ensure that everyone internally is on-board with what the brand image is and make sure that messaging is consistent, whether online, via SMS or mobile or offline. Otherwise, it will spiral out of control, falling flat and seeming disingenuous to the target audience."

Active Cocreators (New) vs. Passive Consumers (Old)

So you've got an active bunch of brand advocates engaged in your brand through your social media channels. What do you do now?

Our research uncovered the Millennial generation's desire for personal success and accomplishment. We'll go into this finding in more detail in Chapter 5, but just know for now that their quest for success can also help drive successful engagement with your brand if done the right way, as Jacqueline Anderson explains.

"Satisfy the Millennials' desire to have something— accomplishments to show their friends or colleagues in the workplace. They will be eager to speak up about your brand on your behalf."

How best to do that? Allow them to cocreate products, and you'll win a brand advocate for life. One organization that has taken this strategy to heart is Babson College, which you'll read about in the following case study.

CASE STUDY: Student-Taught Courses Get Rave Reviews from College Peers

Who?	Babson College
What?	Founded in 1919, Babson has differentiated itself from its peers through its focus on

entrepreneurship training, offering its four-year undergraduates numerous experiential learning opportunities in addition to the more traditional liberal arts curriculum.

"We've led with the notion of being able to live entrepreneurially on campus at the same time they're learning. But students also need to have critical thinking skills that the classic liberal arts curriculum provides," explains Babson's president, Len Schlesinger. "This and our entrepreneurial method are complementary logics and need to be taught, as our students need to develop the capacity of what my colleagues would call [being] 'cognitively ambidextrous' but what I call 'effortlessly bilingual.'"

It's been a successful approach for the school, with 96 percent of its graduates finding jobs upon graduation. Yet, Babson recently realized, the school could be doing more for its students in terms of offering courses that are relevant to the real world.

"There are things like iPhone or iPad app development that our faculty just doesn't have an expertise in," Schlesinger says.

So how did the school address the issue? By turning to its students and asking them not only to help develop the courses but to teach them as well.

How? In the spring of 2012, the school officially kicked off its senior-led seminar series, offering five-week seminars on everything from app

development for entrepreneurs to
the food truck industry. Selected
by faculty for their unique topics,
content, and a well-thought-out
agenda, the free seminars were
taught by Babson seniors, and,
although not for academic credit,
the courses showed up on students'
transcripts.

"Imagine the great questions you will get from those
who review your transcript and see that you took something on the food-truck industry or on corporate social
responsibility," said Dennis Hanno, Babson's dean and
vice provost of the graduate school, in the letter announc-
ing the seminars to students.

Hanno was right. According to Spencer Hughes, the
student who taught the food truck seminar, his course
made a great impression on his current employer and
garnered some unexpected perks. "There isn't a 'how to'
guide to running a food truck (at least not yet), so I was
really starting from scratch when I was putting the course
together. Because my story was featured in the *Boston
Globe*, I now get phone calls [from] people wanting to
hire me as a consultant on how to run their food truck,"
laughs Hughes, who graduated from Babson in 2012.
"It definitely helped me during the interview process,
because it gave me a great story to tell."

Impact?   The student-taught seminars filled
up quickly and got rave reviews from
undergrads and MBA students alike,

and the popular program is slated to continue.

"The seminars will definitely be offered again next year," says Hanno. "In fact, an alumni family was so impressed with them that they offered to financially support them for a few years. I expect we will have even more students interested in teaching them—and in taking them."

"Instead of being rigid and afraid, brands need to let go of the reins a bit and let their consumers, those not content with being passive any longer, help make some of their brand marketing decisions," says Joe Cox. "Who better than your most influential fans and advocates to help you extract the emotional draw, especially when they will to do it for free?"

As you've already learned, Millennials are more than happy to accept the offer.

How best to sum up this chapter? No matter what tactic you choose to take when it comes to engaging with the Millennials, any positive effect it has on your relationship today will have a positive effect on your bottom line tomorrow.

CHAPTER 4: **KEY TAKEAWAYS**

▸ **Millennials spend more time producing and uploading online content than non-Millennials.** Turn them into brand advocates by engaging your key influencers in a conversation that feels authentic and genuine.

▸ **Not all young people want to be friends with brands.** Recent research on younger Millennials found that almost half do not believe brands should have a social presence. This calls for a "listening" strategy—a more nuanced approach to engaging with Millennials online. Rather than bombarding Millennials with brand messages, listen first and then engage after a thorough understanding of their wants and needs is acquired.

▸ **Millennials value relationship building.** While many companies attempt to engage Millennials in a one-time effort, long-lasting relationships go a long way with this generation. Invest in Millennials, and Millennials will invest in you and your brand.

▸ **Millennials are already talking about you.** If you are selling a product or service, chances are, Millennials are already talking about your brand. Find out where those conversations are happening and who your advocates already are, and leverage their affinity by engaging with these advocates, who can later be activated.

➤ **Create a well-rounded engagement strategy.** Employ all the facets of the participation economy. Capture Millennial interest with thought-provoking content. Push this content onto relevant platforms where Millennials are voicing their opinions. Brands must engage Millennials on multiple levels through a well-defined strategy.

Make Them Look Good Among Their Peers

I definitely care what my friends think, and that plays into the items I purchase or the things I do. I ask for advice or reviews of products, and I do a lot of shopping with my friends to observe what they're buying.
— Caroline W., 28, Kansas City, Missouri

The definition of *expert* has drastically changed for the majority of Millennials like Caroline. Professional experience and/or academic credentials aren't the only attributes that qualify someone as an expert.

Anyone with firsthand experience—especially a close friend or peer—can serve as a go-to (and often superior) source for recommendations on brands, products, and services. Indeed, according to a study by Bazaarvoice, 84 percent of Millennials report that user-generated content (UGC) on company websites has at least some influence on what they buy, compared to 70 percent of Baby Boomers. Interestingly, according to the study, the top five purchases Millennials won't make without user-generated content are major electronics (44 percent), cars (40 percent), hotels (39 percent), travel accommodations (32 percent), and credit cards (29 percent).[1]

Not surprisingly, the study recommends that brands put consumer opinions front and center. Because Millennials like to share via social media, companies should optimize everything from mobile to tablet devices in order to facilitate word-of-mouth buzz.

Millennial stat

Eighty-four percent of Millennials report that user-generated content (UGC) on company websites has at least some influence on what they buy, compared to 70 percent of Baby Boomers.

According to a Center for Media research brief, "[Millennials] are not simply looking for feedback from their immediate social/family circle, but looking for input from other shoppers in similar life-situations for assistance in making smart purchase decisions."[2]

Millennials also turn to their social networks for help in making major life decisions. According to the same Bazaarvoice study, Millennials are three times as likely as non-Millennials to turn to their social channels to get opinions on the products and services they buy. Indeed, Millennials are 44 percent more likely than Boomers to trust experts (who happen to be strangers).[3] Take Caroline, for instance. She was not that much of a health nut until a few years ago when she began frequenting a local farmers market. It was there that she discovered the localvore movement—the growing trend toward eating more locally grown and produced foods to support the community and for overall greater health benefits. "That is where I started to become more educated about how far food travels to get to plate," Caroline says.

To delve deeper into the issue, Caroline began following localvore proponents' blogs. Suddenly, she began questioning her own health and lifestyle habits. Was she exercising enough? Eating the right foods?

Before she knew it, Caroline was inspired to exercise more and make healthier food choices, thanks to what she'd learned from the bloggers, some but not all of whom she knew personally. What they all had in common was that they, too, had been on their own weight-loss journeys, giving them firsthand knowledge of what it takes to achieve a healthy lifestyle. No degree required. With this advice came recommendations on products and services that could help Caroline in her quest to get (and stay) healthy and fit.

"I regularly ate yogurt like Yoplait for breakfast until [I] heard about Fage and the benefits of Greek yogurt from a blogger who endorsed their 0 percent fat version and talked about the high protein content. My personal trainer was always on me about eating more protein, so that caught my eye," says Caroline. "It was a great suggestion, especially her tip to add cinnamon to help with its weird consistency and taste. Now it has become a huge staple in my diet. I can eat it for a snack, and it's just perfect. It's 100 calories, low in carbs and sugar, and high in protein, keeping me very full."

In less than a year, thanks to advice and inspiration she received from this support network and from her own efforts, Caroline lost 50 pounds.

"It really became an important resource and support system for me because they knew what I was going through, and they provided me with a lot of valuable information because they had experienced the same challenges I dealt with," Caroline says. "Who knew that an interest in local farming could have such a positive trickle-down effect?"

To tap into their interest in seeking expert opinions on what they buy, the Bazaarvoice study recommends organizing consumer opinions by social and interest graphs. "Serve up the opinions of everyone in a shoppers' social graph right in the purchase path—so it's easy to see what friends think. And also show opinions from other consumers like them, based on your shopper's interests," the study recommends.[4]

Hyperconnected and Always On the Go

So where exactly did this openness to nontraditional sources of *expert* advice and information come from?

First of all, there simply are more sources of info out there. The reach and accessibility of social media and the proliferation of mobile devices have amplified the voice of individuals. Indeed, platforms like Yelp feature online and mobile forums for individuals to rate a variety of restaurants and services. Thanks to these sites, everyone can now be a critic or expert—broadcasting their opinions and viewpoints wherever and whenever they want. And these very same tools give consumers like Caroline the chance to discover, follow, interact with, and learn from a wider variety of sources—especially their peers—than ever before.

Because Millennials are more likely to share and create content, as our research identified, you'll find many Millennials serving as experts for people like Caroline. Messages that resonate go viral, spreading like wildfire through blogs, user reviews, retweets, and online forum discussions.

While consumers of all ages have access to these information-gathering tools, Millennials are more inclined to use them. Why? Well for one, they have more friends they can turn to online. As we explained in Chapter 1, they have twice the number of friends on social networks. Our research found that they also have a deeper level of engagement and multiple points of contact with their connections throughout the day.

Thus, it's no surprise that *crowdsourcing*—tapping into the collective intelligence of the public or one's peer group, as Janelle did when she started her search for a new car (see Chapter 1)—has become a powerful information-gathering *and* decision-making tool for Millennials, even while they are shopping. This point is highlighted in Figure 5-1.

MILLENNIALS SHOP DIFFERENTLY

Attitudes, channel preferences, and shopping behaviors differ from older generations

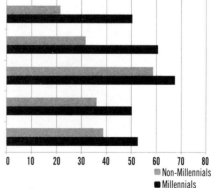

Source: Barkley, The Boston Consulting Group, and Service Management Group, "American Millennials: Deciphering the Enigma Generation," September 2011.

Figure 5-1 An overview of Millennial shopping habits.

*connect w/ other
members is crucial*

Sephora and other retailers are already beginning to build their strategies around these findings, encouraging shoppers to access user reviews via their mobile websites. Taking it one step further, the most exciting opportunity here is for companies to listen to these conversations and then build a strategy that inserts Millennials into the conversations as experts.

Information Hungry

Another contributing factor to their openness to a diverse range of "expert" opinions is Millennials' information-hungry nature, leading them to consult multiple sources, especially in their social circles, as illustrated in Figure 5-2.

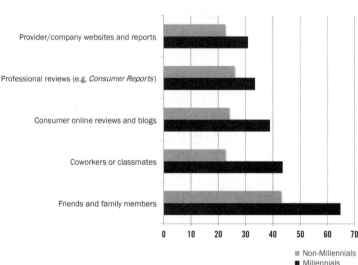

MILLENNIALS SHOP COLLABORATIVELY

They rely more on input from social circles in making product decisions

Source: Barkley, The Boston Consulting Group, and Service Management Group, "American Millennials: Deciphering the Enigma Generation," September 2011.

Figure 5-2 Millennials seek input while shopping.

Findings from other studies on the subject back this up. When making brand decisions in the store, Millennials are 262 percent more likely than the average shopper to be influenced by smartphone apps, 247 percent more likely to be influenced by blogs or social networking sites, and 216 percent more likely to be influenced by in-store touch screen displays, according to research from SymphonyIRI.[5]

While this lengthy consultation process may slow down the decision-making process a bit, Millennials wouldn't have it any other way. Simply stated, they want to ensure they are making the best decision possible.

Millennial stat

Millennials are 262 percent more likely than the average shopper to be influenced by smartphone apps, 247 percent more likely to be influenced by blogs or social networking sites, and 216 percent more likely to be influenced by in-store touch screen displays.

"Before making a major purchase decision, I always ask for my friends' input. If it's something they've bought or used previously, who better than them to know if it works," says Caroline. "I also pay attention to advertising or write-ups in magazines or online. And if I can, I'll try to test out new products, and if I like them, I'll immediately switch over and make that my 'brand of choice.'"

Millennials are also more likely to share their purchases with friends *after* the purchase was made. The Sprint "Mobile Moment of Truth" study found that, compared to older Americans, Millennials are more likely to use a smartphone after shopping to share what they purchased with friends. See Figure 5-3.

Millennials are slightly more active than Older Shoppers AFTER shopping, sharing their purchase, and writing a product review

Q: Which of these ways have you used your smartphone AFTER shopping while in a store?

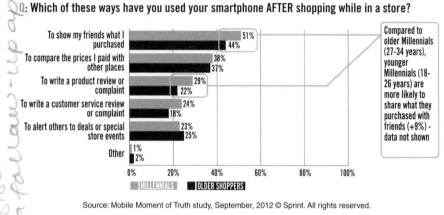

Figure 5-3 Millennial smartphone usage after shopping in store.

While the right brand advocates can be influential, the wrong ones can be detrimental. As Joe Cox, Barkley's social media director, puts it: "Millennials have an amazing nose for bullshit, but they're complete suckers for genuine passion and transparency."

Two good examples are Britney Spears for Pepsi and Jennifer Aniston for Smartwater. They are both megastars and are getting paid a ton of money, but the difference between them is that *Pepsi picked Britney* because she was popular with its target youth market, but *Jennifer picked Smartwater* because it was a product that she openly used daily before she became a spokesperson for the product. She was pictured in lots of magazines drinking it and even talked about it in interviews. She was a true brand advocate, so it made sense for her to represent it.

The following case study illustrates how a 127-year-old brand was able to reinvent itself and attract Millennials by tapping this insight.

CASE STUDY: Brand Reinvention: Using Influencers to Reach a New Generation of Consumers[6]

Who?

Jarden Home Brands and Ball® brand home canning and Fresh Preserving[7]

What?

Canning has grown in popularity over the past two years as consumers try to eat fresh, local products. Concerns about the ingredients that go into the foods consumers eat, along with a need to control the process, drove this trend. However, misconceptions about canning regarding time, complex processes, and safety have prevented many people with the desire to learn to can from trying. Jarden Home Brands wanted to dispel the misconceptions and make the Ball® home canning brand relevant to a new generation of canners.

How?

Jarden Home Brands deployed an integrated media strategy of endorsement with a fresh word-of-mouth twist in the first year of the campaign to reinvigorate the 127-year-old Ball® home canning brand. Jarden Home Brands integrated the Ball® home canning brand into a recipe segment on *The Martha Stewart Show* (a popular show with the brand's target audience) in which Martha shared her favorite jam recipe that she canned using Ball® brand jars and equipment. For Martha's one-thousandth episode, 1,000 Ball® brand jars were displayed on the set along with special events. In the *Food Network Magazine,* a three-page advertorial spread was created in collaboration with popular and well-respected food editor Sara Copeland that highlighted how canning captures the summer season's best fruits and veggies. In addition, house parties, online consumer endorsements, events with well-known canners and cookbook authors, Can It Forward Day, and special events at farmers markets helped spread the word. Building on the success of this campaign in year two, through digital integration and endorsements, Jarden Home Brands introduced a new kitchen appliance for making jam.

Impact

A large advertorial campaign in *Martha Stewart Living* and *Whole Living* magazines reached

15 million influential tastemakers in a single month. On the MarthaStewart.com website, custom rich-media units and photo galleries enjoyed interaction rates as high as 24.45 percent, leading to a MIN Online 2012 Best of the Web award. By seeking endorsements from food experts such as Martha Stewart and Sarah Copeland and leveraging their collective influence across multiple platforms—TV, print, digital, social media, and experiential events—Jarden Home Brands reestablished Ball® brand home canning products as the category leader with its core audience and attracted a new generation of enthusiastic do-it-yourself food lovers.

Two interesting points about this case study. First, not only were the selected brand advocates important to the success of the campaign (although some might raise an eyebrow at the selection of Martha Stewart, she is still considered to be a leading expert in the canning and crafting space, even among Millennials), but product placement was a key component of this campaign as well. Online subscription-cosmetics service Birchbox (which you'll read more about in Chapter 6) teamed up with the CW Network's hit TV series *Gossip Girl* to give subscribers an exclusively branded *Gossip Girl* box (filled with *Gossip Girl*–inspired items and beauty tips from the show's fashion and makeup gurus) as their monthly delivery in May. But the promotion wasn't just about the show's logo getting slapped on the outside of the box or Birchbox popping up in the hands of one of the show's characters. Birchbox's cofounders, Katia Beauchamp and Hayley Barna, who also happen to be Millennials, say this is only the beginning of what's in store for brand partnerships and product placement.

"Gone are the days of slyly slipping a Coke into the refrigerator in movies and expecting consumers to instantly crave the bubbly beverage," according to a *Young Entrepreneur* article about the *Gossip Girl*–Birchbox mashup.[8] Instead, savvy Millennial consumers will reward brands that offer something unique and special.

Gotta Look Good!

So we know that Millennials seek out advice from their friends online in greater numbers than non-Millennials. The interesting question here is *why?*

According to our research, the answer is pretty straightforward: Millennials report gaining a psychological boost from getting *and* giving advice, and they report being influenced by their peers in greater numbers than non-Millennials, as noted in Chapter 1.

This stems from the fact that "Millennials care deeply about their personal brand and others' perception of it and their life choices perhaps more than any generation before it," says Christine Barton, partner at BCG and coauthor of our study. "Engagement in brand choices is crafted to reflect positively on and build their personal brand."

A report from The Futures Company puts it in a historical context: "Boomers valued exclusiveness; for Millennials, it is all about inclusiveness. The appeal of a product has already become tied to the number of friends who like it or recommend it [on Facebook]."[9]

Or by how many peers say, "Wow, that's cool!"

Megan, whom you met in Chapter 3, says she is usually a private and serious person. But her desire to be seen as "cutting edge" by her peers led her to be one of the very first consumers to own an iPhone, despite the high cost of the device and the expense of having to break her old carrier contract to make the switch.

"All of my friends were saying, 'Oh my God, is that an iPhone? That's so cool.' Or I'd be waiting for a plane and would catch people looking at me. I definitely felt special being the first to own an iPhone back then because it was so new and there was no other smartphone in the market," says Megan. "I usually hate it when people look at me because I really don't want to be in [the] limelight. I just want people to know I'm different, and the iPhone helped me achieve a cutting edge image."

This was all accomplished without her having to say one word. The takeaway for brands? You have to effectively communicate how your product reflects positively on these consumers.

Brands like Apple have tapped into something special, creating a line of products that have a perceived elite status that gets immediately transferred to the consumer upon purchase. Millennials, in particular, are devoted to this brand not only for its "cool" factor but also for some not-so-obvious reasons, as this *Washing-*

ton Post education columnist points out: "Perhaps it's the Apple college discount that allows students to justify spending more on an iPod than on a regular MP3 player. Or maybe it's the peer pressure. Or the design. Or the desire to be different than your PC-loving parents. Or a dedication dating back to childhood."[10]

Let's home in on that dedication that dates back to childhood. Millennials grew up with Apple, witnessing the transformation of the brand in their lives such that Apple products often served as "mile markers" in the form of junior high or high school graduation gifts. In turn, Apple grew up with this generation as well, contributing to the brand's astute understanding of what Millennials value most and its uncanny ability to tailor products to specifically fit their needs.

People Care About What I Say, Where I Am, and What I'm Doing

Related to this desire to look cool among their peers, Millennials believe there is an audience for every minute detail of every action and thought, and they will broadcast these details to their network. If you've ever seen a tweet or Facebook status update from a Millennial-age friend, child, or sibling, you've likely rolled your eyes a time or two.

Dr. Jean Twenge's book *Generation Me* goes into great detail on this "egocentric, image-driven" view of the world, whereby everyone (or every Millennial) sees him- or herself as important, even celebrity-like.[11]

Exacerbating this image-driven view is the pressure Millennials place on themselves to be (or at least look like) a success, leading them to spend hours crafting and perfecting their Facebook profiles. See Figure 5-4.

This is just really interesting

SUCCESS AND STATUS MATTER

Success is a matter of hard work, and status is worth the price

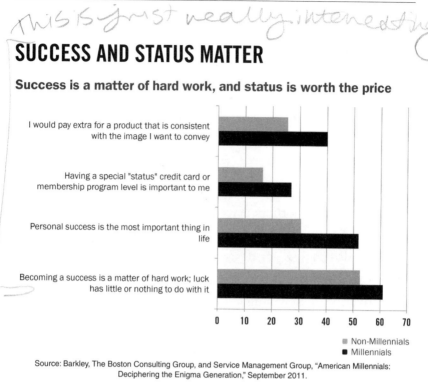

Source: Barkley, The Boston Consulting Group, and Service Management Group, "American Millennials: Deciphering the Enigma Generation," September 2011.

Figure 5-4 Millennials value success and status.

Compared to older generations, Millennials feel that their success is in their own hands. As one Millennial put it in his response to our survey: "I am successful because I have my hands in everything, from working on my own website, writing for our school paper, interning at a prestigious PR firm, studying abroad this summer, getting good grades, having private tutors, worked for an investment firm and passed my Series 6 exam on the first try, and being healthy by means of working out regularly." Frankly, reading his list of activities wears us out!

Let's return for a moment to Caroline, who is a frequent Yelp .com reviewer. She also keeps a personal blog, where she reviews movies. Though she isn't getting paid for her work, this activity allows her to "have an excuse to watch movies," something that she loves doing anyway, as it has given her a voice and special status among her friends. "This gave me the perfect excuse to do it," she says. "People now come at me with suggestions on movies. It's been a lot of fun. If Roger Ebert wanted me to be his best friend, I wouldn't complain."

Companies like Yelp, with its "Elite" status designation for the best reviewers, and Klout, which ranks people based on their social influence on others, have successfully used the insight that personal success and status matter to these consumers. How can your brand recognize or designate importance to its best advocates? It's a significant consideration when it comes to engaging and activating these young consumers.

Similarly, through platforms like Foursquare, which allows users to check in to various locations and share with their followers, Millennials have yet another opportunity to cultivate a specific image to the world around them. The notion of Millennials striving for status goes a step further on the Foursquare site: Users can compete with one another to claim reign over a particular location. It allows its most frequent users to become "Mayor" of a particular location, creating an opportunity for the site's heaviest users to brag about it to their followers. Having surpassed 20 million users and over 2 billion check-ins, with 21 percent of collegians and 13 percent of high schoolers regularly using the site to check in, according to Ypulse research, Foursquare has tapped into something special among members of the Millennial generation.[12]

So What Does This All Mean?

We've covered a lot of territory in this chapter. But what does it mean to your organization?

To recap, a report from The Futures Company summarized the peer influence factor best: "For Millennials, everything begins and ends with social connections. The team dynamic is the defining characteristic of their generational experience. It is also the common aspect of everything else that characterizes the millennial experience. Thus, friends are a central element of [a brand's] success."[13]

Our study findings elevate the relevance and magnify the impact of marketing tools such as word of mouth and advocacy. Millennials care what their social circles and influencers think. As a result of their online ties, they are empowered to participate and engage in the process of building brands as well as tearing them down. Thus, companies must vigilantly monitor what is being said about their brands—and be willing to participate in the conversation.

Also, as group activity drives increased frequency and spend across categories, there is an opportunity for brands to adopt location-based services (for example, Foursquare) to capitalize on this trend. The same report from the Futures Company elucidates: "The status of a car, for example, may not be any of the traditional cues, but rather the number of friends who own the same make and model. The reputation of something as commonplace as a carton of milk might be enhanced by seeing pictures of friends on the carton or on the Web site or mentioned in a company blog. The street view of a house may soon be less important than the 'friends view' of a house. And so forth."[14]

Since peers have the most influence over Millennials, brands must figure out how to elevate their voices. And because Millennials greatly depend on the recommendations and comments of their friends in both the on- and offline worlds, this begs the need for companies to think more holistically about strategies and technologies that work across platforms.

CHAPTER 5: **KEY TAKEAWAYS**

▸ **Millennials have redefined what it means to be an expert.** In years past, certain credentials were needed for a person to be qualified as an expert. Today, professional experience and academic credentials need not be requirements. Millennials are considered experts simply for being born in this generation. Capitalize on their knowledge, and tap into their insights.

▸ **Millennials have larger social networks.** As a result, they have more "experts" they can turn to for firsthand advice on major purchase decisions. Elevate the voices of standout Millennial experts to generate more awareness and affinity for your brand.

▸ **Millennials have more platforms to choose from.** Yes, Millennials have larger social networks that provide an increased amount of resources for decision making. But Millennials also have more platforms from which to garner information, including social media, mobile apps, and the Web. Find the right platform or combination of platforms for your brand to reach Millennials.

▸ **Millennials are heavily influenced by their peers.** Given the influence of their social circles and people who are "just like them," companies will need to revisit whether current brand endorsers are credible and effective with this audience. While the right brand advocates can be very influential, the wrong ones can be detrimental.

➤ **Thanks to their large networks and strong social ties, Millennials are empowered to participate and engage in the process of building brands as well as tearing them down.** Companies must be vigilant in monitoring what is being said about their brands and be willing to participate in the conversation.

CHAPTER 6

Design a Sense of Fun and Adventure

I've always enjoyed the Olympic movement and enjoy watching all of the sports—whether very traditional like luge, bobsled or skeleton. After college graduation, I moved to Lake Placid, [New York], to work as a marketing assistant for the U.S. Luge Association and team. Once I moved, the skeleton coach asked me to try skeleton, so I did. It was a great experience—very fun, thrilling and borderline dangerous.

—Brittany M., 34, Harrisburg, Pennsylvania

No matter what age you are, a jet-setter lifestyle can sound like fun. Who wouldn't want Brittany's flexibility to make a big move and follow a passion without the guarantee of a long-term pay-off?

Of course, not everyone can up and move or travel the world without a care. Jobs, kids, and everyday commitments keep most of us grounded to some extent.

Millennial stat

Millennials more than non-Millennials reported a desire to visit every continent in their lifetime (70 percent vs. 48 percent) and travel abroad as much as possible (75 percent vs. 52 percent).

It should come as no surprise that, due in part to their life stage, Millennials express an overwhelming desire for adventure, and they pursue these opportunities as if they are keeping a scorecard and checking off experiences as they go. Whether they accomplish it by traveling as much as possible or through a willingness to expose themselves to a certain amount of danger in pursuit of excitement, our study found that Millennials have a singular quest: achieving a variety of experiences, as Figure 6-1 reveals.

"I live my life doing what I want to do when I want to," Brittany says when asked to explain her philosophy, adding, "My husband and I like to travel and strive to do it as much as we can. I love going fast on roller coasters, zip lines or anything. We live our lives for adventure."

While she recently became a first-time mom (which has grounded her for a bit), she is already making plans for her next adventure—a trip to Europe with her husband.

"We're already planning to go somewhere fun next summer like Europe," says Brittany. "If we want to go somewhere, we'll figure out how to get there, as much as we can afford to do it. Life is too short to not have some fun."

Not all Millennials are getting to pursue the laissez-faire lifestyle as much as they'd like, due in part to lingering effects of the economic downturn. However, their general sense of adventurousness still manifests itself in their interest in other cultures, exotic foods, and novel activities that they can enjoy closer to home. Case in point: After growing up on mac and cheese, Brittany can't get enough bulgogi at her favorite Korean restaurant in town.

MILLENNIALS SEEK A BROADER RANGE OF ACTIVITIES

Millennials have a global view of travel, enjoy everything from opera to rock climbing

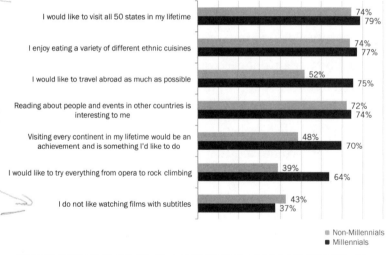

Source: Barkley, The Boston Consulting Group, and Service Management Group, "American Millennials: Deciphering the Enigma Generation," September 2011.

Figure 6-1 Millennials seek adventure.

But wait. Eating Korean food in Pennsylvania seems a lot different from eating Korean food during a trip to South Korea. Do these other non-travel-related experiences also qualify as "adventure" in the eyes of a Millennial? They sure do, as Philadelphia-based Jiate Zhang, age 26, explains: "People tend to think of the world traveler, or thrill seeker, or some other romanticized definitions of what being adventurous should be. For me, it's more about curiosity and the willingness to try new things. I've done a lot of seemingly random and disconnected things, and yet looking back, it's always curiosity that has been the driving force."

A brand that can capitalize on this desire for new experiences and a taste for adventure by differentiating its offering will do well with Millennials. Birchbox is a great example of a company that is satisfying this adventuresome spirit in the cosmetics space. Launched in 2010 by two female Harvard Business School grads, the company's mission is to help women "cut through the clutter of the beauty world to find products that really work for them."[1]

Birchbox is an online cosmetics company that curates and delivers a monthly supply of high-end beauty product samples to subscribers for just $10 a month. Customers simply create a profile on the Birchbox website, answering various questions about skin type, hair color, and the types of products they would like to receive. Then, at the beginning of each month, a customized package is shipped directly to each customer. It's as if every subscriber had a personal stylist working just for her.

Initially, the site was limited to 660 members who were recruited through word of mouth. Since then, it has enjoyed exponential growth in membership and sales. Birchbox recently reported more than 100,000 monthly subscribers! It has even begun the process of creating a Birchbox for men and has acquired a similar venture based out of Paris, called JolieBox.

Described as a "leading pioneer in subscription e-commerce,"[2] Birchbox is having great success with this endeavor *and* is especially popular among Millennials, who enjoy the thrill of getting a "surprise" delivery of beauty goodies each month. As many bloggers have described it, Birchbox is like "Christmas every month."[3]

Birchbox integrates adventure and fun into the brand with its customized e-commerce delivery model. And to top it off, Birchbox offers a program whereby subscribers can accumulate points through online purchases, friend referrals, and product reviews. After they accrue 100 points, they receive a discount on a full-price item.

Given the company's quick success, it's no wonder that similar personal styling sites are popping up to help consumers by "editing down all the noise," as Birchbox cofounder Katia Beauchamp commented.[4] Using shoppers' personal style and brand preferences as identified in proprietary surveys, e-mails, and phone queries, these companies are making specific-to-the-individual recommendations on everything from clothes and shoes to nail polish and jewelry.

Millions of consumers are flocking to sites like Birchbox and ShoeDazzle, which sends its 13 million members e-mails with a link to its "personalized boutique" of shoe styles every month. BaubleBar, which sells jewelry, doesn't use surveys but employs a SWAT—Service With Accessorizing Talent—team to answer customer questions via e-mail or phone about how to pair jewelry or put together an outfit around a new purchase.

"Instead of 'Build it and they will come,' these e-commerce merchants practice 'Personalize and push it and they will shop,'" said Nita Rollins, a trends expert for digital marketing agency Resource, as quoted in the same article.[5]

Market Disrupters Win Big

Birchbox and its fellow personal styling sites are good examples of *disruptive marketing*—the tactic of "breaking through the noise with a disruptive idea or a disruptive message supported by an underlying authentic persona or product"[6]—which has proven effective with Millennials over the past several years. By imbuing its very business model with a heavy dose of the fun factor, Birchbox has broken through the already cluttered beauty industry to offer something unique for consumers.

TOMS Shoes is another brand that has disrupted an industry with its adventurous take on doing business. When asked to name a brand that they love or one that truly "gets" Millennials, many of our Millennial-age survey respondents named TOMS as their favorite, thanks to its innovative "buy one, give one" (BOGO) business model, which generates a free pair of shoes for a child in need for every pair sold.

"TOMS Shoes inspire[s] me. It's not about cause marketing with them. It's part and parcel to what they do. It's inspired me to do the same with my company, which provides lower-cost, fixed-rate student loans through an alumni and investor funded platform," says David Klein, CEO of Common Bond, a start-up that applies crowdsourcing to student loans. "For every degree that is fully funded through our platform, we are funding the education of a student in [a] developing country for a full year. Some have dubbed us the 'TOMS Shoes of education.' It's an honor we humbly accept."

Klein's sentiments are shared by many of the Millennials we interviewed for this book. Never before had a shoe company introduced such a concept. But as a result of the success of TOMS founder Blake Mycoskie's BOGO model, you can now find many examples of the concept (or some version of it) across a wide variety of product category lines. What began as a line of strange-looking shoes worn mainly by the socially conscious Millennial generation consumers (more about that in the final chapter of this book) can now be found on the feet of men and women ranging from the toddler at the playground to the business executive on vacation.

Want another example? In the following case study, you'll learn how Millennial entrepreneur Michael Dubin disrupted the sluggish men's shaving category by injecting a little dose of *fun* to help him take on the goliaths.

CASE STUDY: Market Disruptor Goes Big-Time Thanks to Viral Video and a Savvy Business Model

Who?	Dollar Shave Club
What?	A new e-commerce razors and blades home-delivery service wakes up the sleepy men's shaving product category.
How?	In this category, Procter & Gamble's Gillette brand is the clear behemoth, with more than 66 percent share of the $12 billion-plus market.[7] Yet P&G's more traditional and conservative approach to advertising—enlisting celebrities André 3000, Gael García Bernal, and Adrien Brody to serve as brand ambassadors in its most recent

campaign[8]—had long seemed stale to Millennial Michael Dubin.

Dubin, an entrepreneurially minded digital marketer by trade and a student of comedy at night, was looking for the right opportunity to launch his own product line and brand. He just wasn't sure what product category to go after first.

After a chance meeting with a friend's father-in-law, who said he had the 411 on high-quality cheap razors made in Asia, Dubin knew what he wanted to do: launch an e-commerce company that would go after the men's shaving market.

Within just a few months, and with one hilarious video that went viral on YouTube,[9] Dubin successfully launched the Dollar Shave Club, an e-commerce razor and blade home-delivery service.

"You'll find that the people who really speak to [Millennial consumers] are not traditional folks that have been speaking to consumers on behalf of these big brands. It goes beyond being a celebrity," says Dubin. "The smartest thing we did was to feature just ordinary people talking about a common gripe. And we delivered a laugh. We didn't have to use any celebrities or spend any money, and we made this awesome video that really speaks to these consumers. I'm just a middle class white dude from Philadelphia!"

Maybe not middle class any longer.

Impact?　　While the company has not shared sales figures to date, it has managed to raise $1 million in seed funding from major Silicon Valley venture capital firms and has signed up thousands of previously disgruntled shaving consumers across the country.

Although the company wasn't specifically out to target Millennials, these consumers were the first to pick up on the video, *and thanks to their many online connections,* they were key to it going viral, says Dubin.

"They helped bring it to the attention of a larger group of male consumers who, too, were pissed off having to waste time buying and spending so much for their razors."

The main point of this case study? When it comes to marketing to Millennials, innovation and a little dose of humor win out.

Comedy Natives

As the Dollar Shave Club case study so perfectly points out, humor is a key ingredient in satisfying the Millennial consumer's desire for fun and adventure, especially among the advertiser-coveted 18- to 34-year-old male demographic.

Recent research backs this up. Humor is the lens through which young men view others, according to findings from a 2012 study conducted by Comedy Central.[10] When it comes to sizing people up, comedy trumps even music, sports, and personal style.

Even more telling, 88 percent of respondents to the Comedy Central survey said their self-definition was highly influenced by their sense of humor. Almost three-quarters believe humorous people are better liked, and more than half said they sent out funny videos to make a positive impression on someone else. An online survey of 2,000 respondents by Nielsen Entertainment Television essentially found the same.[11]

Comedy is intrinsically intertwined with Millennials' identities, according to Tanya Giles, the executive vice president of Strategic Insights and Research at Viacom Media Networks.[12] Not surprisingly, several of Comedy Central's shows, such as *Tosh.0, The Daily Show with Jon Stewart,* and *The Colbert Report,* score high marks with Millennial men due to their heavy dose of comedy.

Advertisers are getting into the game as well. By now, you've probably heard of the popular trend dubbed "Movember"[13] that encourages men to grow mustaches during the month of November to raise awareness of prostate cancer. This event was created by a group of young men from Australia.[14]

To support this cause, Gillette launched an annual campaign and social media effort on its Twitter account and Facebook page, where interested participants could download the "Capture Your Mo" app, which enabled men to upload a photo and create a time-lapse video of their growing mustaches each day throughout the month. At the end of "Movember," participants received a special video highlighting the growth of their glorious mustaches.

To give an added boost to the effort and cause, for every picture that a participant uploaded to his time-lapse video during the month of November, Gillette donated a dollar, up to a total of $50,000, to support programs run by Movember and its men's health partner, Prostate Cancer Foundation. As an extra deal sweetener, the most shareable "Mo' Growth" videos were selected by a panel of internal style judges and featured in rotation on the Times Square billboard in New York City.

We suspected that the campaign would be a hit among Millennial men, who enjoy a good laugh for a good cause (more on this subject in Chapter 7). Gillette not only introduced elements of entertainment and adventure into its own brand but also created a way to shed light on a serious issue in a fun and interesting way.

Generation Innovation

A Millennial's quest for adventure can even translate to the working world. For instance, many Millennials are becoming entrepreneurs in adulthood (some famously doing so while they're still in college), exercising their willingness to take risks in hopes of a more interesting and fulfilling career than they would have had otherwise if they had stuck to a traditional career path.

Michael Dubin, the Dollar Shave Club entrepreneur introduced earlier, is a perfect example. After spending a few years working in digital marketing for large media companies, he was ready to set out on his own.

"Entrepreneurship is the most important thing to me," explained Dubin during our interview. "I always wanted to start my own company, even when I was working at Time Inc. on some of their digital properties and trying to start my own company in the shadows."

Entrepreneurship offers the additional benefit of giving Millennials another avenue for acquiring work experience during a bad economy.[15]

To capture the Millennial generation's entrepreneurial drive, MTV has begun to call it "Generation Innovation" in recognition of the proliferation of creators, entrepreneurs, and innovators it has produced.

According to MTV's Nick Shore, who leads the company's research arm, MTV Insights, Millennials will drastically reshape this country in terms of culture and commerce.

"We see a very creative, generative, 'maker' and 'fixer' spirit in the generation," Shore said in a Ypulse interview.[16]

To delve deeper into these questions, MTV's "Generation Innovation" study in 2012 explored the Millennials' creative ethos—what their creative process looks like, what systems they are beginning to reshape and hypothesize about, and what a Millennial-driven world will be like in 20 years. What did they find? The "Generation Innovation" study found that 72 percent of Millennial respondents expressed a desire to create things people love.

"[T]hey are the most educated generation in history, but when they graduate, they aren't finding work," said Shore. "They need to find an outlet for their creativity and resourcefulness."[17]

Given the lack of traditional jobs, Millennials are finding an outlet through their own entrepreneurial endeavors. No matter what they end up creating, Millennials will undoubtedly aim to offer the same sense of fun and adventure they seek from the relationships with brands they shop today.

The one criticism of studying their creative nature is that not every Millennial is actively creating things. Nevertheless, this urge to create represents a cresting tide, in Shore's opinion. As a brand seeking to reach Millennial consumers, consider how you can engage their creativity.[18]

Need an example of a brand that's effectively engaging Millennials' creativity? Well, it just so happens that MTV has taken its own advice. As early as 2008, the company was testing out new ways to enhance its internal creative process that would give Millennial viewers the opportunity to help shape and create programming.

To facilitate an exchange of ideas, MTV launched a community made up of 300 Millennials in the United States, ages 18 to 22, who were asked to offer their insights to the MTV team. This endeavor "allow[ed] them to adjust television and web offerings in real time—altering content and strategies at the speed which their target demands," according to a case study on Communispace, which built and managed the community. The community directly influenced the 2008 Video Music Awards (VMAs). The community members, who provided feedback on the VMA promo campaign in advance of its launch, were credited with providing crucial insights that MTV acted upon, leading to a 26 percent increase in ratings over the prior year. Strategies like this work for MTV because Millennials view the invitation and opportunity to help the brand create something of importance as fun and exciting. As one of the community participants explained: "It's also awesome to know that we influence MTV. It's good having a voice and more importantly, having that voice be heard!"[19]

Sounds like a win-win to us.

The Parent Trap

Before moving on, we have to ask: Just how much of this taste for adventure is life-stage driven and how much is a true generational difference between Millennials and non-Millennials?

The adventure-seeking approach to life—the ability to be spontaneous, take risks, and live in the moment—certainly diminishes the older we get. For instance, our study found that the arrival of children, which brings increased responsibilities and financial obligations, directly impacts the Millennials' quest for adventure via international travel. However, while interest in global travel decreased in Millennials with children, our study found their interest level remains above that of non-Millennials.

What about their always-on-the-go lifestyle? Does having children impact that? Nope. Millennial parents are keenly focused on preventing that from happening. Brands that help them maintain their focus are scoring wins with them.

Take new parents Jake and Annabelle, for example. They made the difficult decision to leave their beloved, fast-paced urban setting of Chicago for a house in the suburbs once their baby girl arrived. Refusing to be banned to the burbs, they frequently make trips into the city—often with their baby in tow—for a taste of the adventure and excitement they left behind.

"I want to show and give my kid as much as I can by taking her out in the city and showing her things I'm interested in," says Jake. "Certainly, we do things within reason and have to make sacrifices like going a little earlier to things. But we've made it clear that we want to bring our child into everything we do, make her an integral part by not leaving her behind with a babysitter like my parents did when they went on a vacation for instance. I definitely think that makes us different from Boomer parents."

And if it takes a village to raise happy and healthy children, it also takes companies and brands that understand and cater to the special needs of this new generation of parents, Jake says.

According to this busy new father, he couldn't live without brands such as Earth's Best and its infant puree pouches that make it easy for him—and his baby—to stay on the go. And it doesn't hurt that all of their products are nutritious and organic.

"Their products are built for convenience," Jake explains. "They truly get the needs of modern day parents, and I appreciate that."

Other brands are also tapping into on-the-go parents' needs. Ella's Kitchen, a baby-enthusiast brand, provides organic, all-natural ingredients in a convenient package that helps alleviate the spills and messes that typically accompany snack time. With bright colors and kid-friendly designs, Ella's Kitchen packaging is enticing to both child and parent.

Annabelle, however, is surprised that more brands, especially restaurants—which often banish them to the back of the room—aren't making more of an effort to cater to parents like her and Jake.

"I can't tell you how many times I've had to enter through the disabled door because the stroller wouldn't fit through the entrance," she says. "And public bathrooms? Forget it. Many still have changing stations only in the women's bathroom and not the men's, so my husband can't do it."

The offering doesn't have to be extravagant. Simple things like having crayons or sippy cups can make a big difference.

"For something as common as having children, you'd think that some companies would cater to us. I'm surprised that many don't. There is a restaurant in town that offers many family-friendly features like sippy cups and crayons, which seem like thoughtless things, but I can't tell you how special it is when we find them. I think we've eaten there 10 times in the past few months. Truly, there is nothing more amazing than when a brand or company makes life easier for you as a parent."

Brands like Earth's Best, Ella's Kitchen, and Annabelle's favorite local restaurant that understand and facilitate a Millennial parent's desire to remain active and on-the-go will do well with this new generation of parents.

So when it comes to winning over Millennial consumers—nonparents and parents alike—seek ways to offer them a sense of adventure and fun through your brand experience. They will reward you with increased loyalty and will even bring friends to the party!

CHAPTER 6: **KEY TAKEAWAYS**

▸ **Millennials define adventure in a variety of ways.** From traveling around the world or within the United States to trying new food, Millennials find adventure in different forms. It can be as exotic as traveling thousands of miles around the globe or simply trying rock climbing. For Millennials, everything is outside of the box and anything is a possibility.

▸ **Millennials crave adventure in large numbers**. While they may not be able to afford to pursue every adventure on their list, brands that capitalize on this desire for new experiences and a taste for adventure by differentiating their offering will do well with this generation of consumers.

▸ **Brands with an older target demographic cannot neglect the Millennial generation, given their size and influence.** The sooner that established brands can begin creating a relationship with Millennial consumers—even if by merely starting a dialogue—the better.

▸ **Adventure can also mean taking risks for Millennials.** This generation identifies opportunity in risk taking. Millennials are a group filled with entrepreneurs and business risk takers. The difference between Millennials and previous generations? The former finds adventure in the midst of risk. Brands can use this notion to their advantage and expand their own brand strategy to increase appeal with Millennials.

▸ **While global travel may decrease with the arrival of children, Millennial parents still want adventure.** Brands that cater to and help facilitate their on-the-go lifestyle will do well.

Don't Give Them a Reason to Cheat on You

I feel loyal to certain brands and I am extremely loyal to TOMS Shoes. I will recommend them to friends and family or complete strangers. For example, I often choose to give them as gifts whenever I can. Why do I love them so much? I love their approach to business—for every pair of shoes they sell, they donate to a child in a developing country. This is a huge reason as to why I am such a loyal customer . . . also they are cute and comfy.

—Courtney W., 25, Kansas City, Missouri

Winning the loyalty of Millennials can seem hard—if not impossible—for many brands these days. But a few, like TOMS Shoes, have managed to tap into something special.

For those not as successful as TOMS, well, you can blame the economy. As many brands come of age during a challenging economic time, the "fiscal prudence practiced by this segment is more intense versus that of the general population," states a SymphonyIRI Consumer Network report.[1]

"The one standout quality about this generation is their frugality," agrees Brand Amplitude's Carol Phillips. "If you're not a millennial, you probably paid too much!"

So just how are they flexing their more fiscally prudent muscles? From at-home beauty care to homemade meals to more self-reliant approaches to healthcare, Millennials are trying to save where they can in greater numbers than other population groups.[2] And because they have to watch what they spend, "deals and steals" have become a part of their money-saving arsenal.

"Millennial shoppers are more heavily influenced by a range of money-saving opportunities versus the population as a whole," according to the SymphonyIRI report, which found that more than half of Millennials are influenced by shopper loyalty discounts as well as traditional coupons.[3]

Our study essentially found the same, uncovering that Millennials seek value and rewards in greater numbers. In fact, nearly half expressed a willingness to go out of their way to shop at stores offering rewards programs. Even more eye-opening: They are willing to switch from favorite brands to those that save them money. The bottom line? A good deal goes a long way with this generation.

Study participant Courtney can attest to the importance of a good deal. Her husband, Paul, is still in school, forcing them to stick to a budget. Restaurants like Granite City Food & Beer, a regional restaurant chain in the Midwest, have quickly become favorites. While Granite City offers "great appetizers and beer selection," according to Courtney, it was the restaurant's Mug

Club rewards points program, which offers special discounts to frequent customers, that sealed the deal.

"We don't go out on date nights all the time, so when we do, it's nice to feel like we're getting our money's worth. Everyone likes getting discounts or upgrades for free," says Courtney, referring to the Mug Club membership. "It's more fun to go out and feel like I'm splurging, even though I'm not."

These special perks make her even more loyal to the brand: "I definitely feel more loyal to a brand when I feel like I'm a part of it and can get all these great deals with a card," she says.

The Price *Needs* to Be Right

Given their affinity for a good deal, it's no surprise that Millennials say *price is the most important factor* when it comes to making a purchase decision.

"Millennials are willing to spend," says Carol Phillips. "But they want a good deal, and will often buy luxury goods off-price at places like T.J.Maxx or outlets. They're like stalkers when it comes to getting a good deal on something they really want."

Not only does price influence brand decisions, it also dictates where they shop, with 86.3 percent of Millennials reporting that having the lowest prices was a first or second attribute choice when deciding at which store to shop.[4] This point is illustrated in Figure 7-1, which provides data from our study that highlights how Millennial women prefer discount retailers.

Mass retailers are their primary destination, but they are much more likely than non-Millennials to shop at discount or off-price clothing stores such as T.J.Maxx and Marshalls, as Phillips points out.

MILLENNIAL WOMEN PREFER DISCOUNT AND SPECIALTY RETAIL

All generations favor mass retailers and department stores

Source: Barkley, The Boston Consulting Group, and Service Management Group, "American Millennials: Deciphering the Enigma Generation," September 2011.

Figure 7-1 Female Millennial shopping preferences.

Some cash-strapped Millennials, bogged down with living expenses and student loan debt, are going beyond discount stores.

More and more frugal Millennials are looking for even cheaper, albeit more alternative, ways to buy clothes. Apparel-swapping websites, apps, and meetups are among the ways Millennials are going about updating their closets. Brad Tuttle writes that Millennials' affinity for this is derived from growing up in a "disposable culture."[5] The clothes aren't necessarily new, but they're new to the consumer. *swaps?*

According to a *Bloomberg* article, Millennials are also saving money by using iPhone apps like PoshMark, which allows users to essentially "shop" in other people's closets. Users can search for a particular item—boots, a purse, other accessories—or they can search another user's entire "closet."[6]

Other Millennials are using savvyswap.com or event-planning websites such as Meetup.com to create clothing swap events. In Washington, D.C., some of these meetups have hundreds of participants.

Wendy Liebmann, chief executive officer of New York–based WSL, told *Bloomberg* in a phone interview that this type of shopping almost comes naturally to Millennials. "This generation has also grown up in an online world of Craigslist and eBay where selling something or swapping something has become somewhat second nature," she said.[7]

Millennials want a good deal, and they don't necessarily care if the items are secondhand. Does this mean Millennials are throwing brand loyalty out the window in the search for a good deal?

What Ever Happened to Brand Loyalty?

When it comes to these bargain-hunting Millennial shoppers, is brand loyalty a thing of the past? Yes and no.

While 43 percent of Millennials prefer to shop the brands they grew up with, 56 percent are willing to switch brands in favor of a good deal, even in the form of a cents-off coupon. On top of that, 63 percent have purchased nonfavorite brands to take advantage of a sale or promotion.[8]

These findings underscore the need for brands to emphasize value.

So far, we have focused on price as an important component of the value equation when marketing to Millennials. Put into practice, private-label programs are one effective way to build loyalty among members of this consumer segment because, as the SymphonyIRI report points out, "These types of programs elevate the value profile of the retailer."[9] It's a smart tactic to take. While it allows companies to use assets that are already available to them, it also provides a path for strengthening their brand identity among cost-conscious Millennials. Just ask Whole Foods Market, which has not only found success as a pioneer of the private-label strategy but also managed to attract Millennials to its stores "in droves."[10] Through its top-performing 365 Everyday Value and 365 Organic Everyday Value brands, the high-end grocer is able to appeal to those price-conscious Millennial shoppers who are also on the hunt for healthier food and organic options that they already know Whole Foods provides. These private-label brands address the needs of bargain-hunting Millennial shoppers who are passionate about healthy foods.

Up the Fun Factor

Another effective loyalty-building strategy is to up the *fun factor* of the brand. As we pointed out in Chapter 6, Millennial shoppers are more likely than others to search out fun retail experiences. The most effective way to do it? Create brand experiences that they value. Millennials expect consumer-centric shopping experiences tailored to their wants and needs.

While JCPenney's "fair and square" pricing strategy might not have caught on with consumers, the brand is now scoring points with Millennials with its store makeovers and in-store experiences. A few years ago, Blair, 26, would never have stepped foot in the store if weren't for the occasional trip with her mom when she was home from college.

"I would only go to Penney's when I was visiting my mom over the holidays. I hated having to go there. They never carried the brands I wanted, and the stores were just a mess," she says.

"I went back to shop recently, and I liked it so much. They've really changed the look of their stores, and it just looks nicer . . . more organized. They even hold town halls in the middle of their stores and offer a free ice cream parlor every now and then. It's nice to see a big retailer like that doing something good for the community."

Not only is Blair shopping there more often; her affinity has inspired her to follow the retailer on Twitter and Facebook to see what it may have up its sleeve.

"I've tweeted at them to let them know I like their changes. I also like following them to know when they are marking stuff down," she says.

To up the fun factor, the store is also ditching cashiers, cash registers, and checkout counters, replacing them with technology solutions and self-checkout options that will make checkout a breeze. And what about the cost savings? They will be reinvested in the company to provide better customer service.[11]

An additional example is Ford Motor Company, which has effectively upped the fun factor to attract Millennial consumers (see sidebar that follows). At the time of printing, JCPenney's former CEO, Myron Ullman, had recently been asked to resume the helm of the company. What impact this event will have on these changes remains to be seen.

CASE STUDY: How One Car Company Stays Ahead of the Curve with Millennials

Who:	Ford Motor Company
What:	Almost half of teens say that, if given a choice, they would rather

have Internet access than a car, according to a 2012 Gartner survey as cited in NYTimes.com.[12]

This news doesn't bode well for carmakers that are already struggling to reach a generation of consumers who don't drive like their parents used to. Just how different are they? U.S. Transportation Department statistics indicate that while 50 percent of 16-year-olds in the United States obtained their first driver's license in 1978, only 30 percent did so in 2008, as cited in New York Times.com.[13]

Okay, so maybe it's for economic reasons (for example, the higher cost of obtaining a license). But it's more complex than that. Another set of Transportation Department statistics note that those who do get a license drive less: 21- to 30-year-olds now drive 8 percent fewer miles than they did in 1995.[14]

Sheryl Connelly, Ford Motor Company's manager of global consumer trends and futuring, says there's another important contributing factor at play. "In the 60s, the car was an iconic symbol of freedom and independence. Making that same correlation today, the cellphone is the symbol of freedom and independence."

A car, according to Connelly, was also "the only thing you could really save for in the 60s. Today, there are a whole host of things—smartphones, games, laptops, tablets—competing for that 16-year-old's limited financial resources. They also have more partners for transportation like bike and Zipcar rental programs, and their parents don't mind carpooling them around."

Despite these competing interests and the Millennial generation's ho-hum interest in cars, Ford still wants to make a connection.

"The population is very large in terms of scale and influence. It's the only generation that is bigger than Baby Boomers," says Connelly. "There are really only two different pathways for Ford to sell to a 16-year-old today—a gateway purchase into adulthood or to replace the cellphone."

Since Millennials won't be trading in their cell phones for a car anytime soon, the challenge for Ford today is clear: The car company must figure out an effective way to connect with consumers who don't think they even need a car today in the hope that they'll choose Ford tomorrow.

How: "If I asked customers what they wanted, they would have said faster horses," Henry Ford famously said.

When devising a marketing strategy for Millennials, this guiding principle still rings true for the car company, Ford's Connelly says. "We try to help shape the marketplace and deliver to consumers things they can't even imagine they'd want today. So what's relevant in the marketplace today may not be what's relevant three years from now.

"It's complicated and tricky because you can't just ask customers 'What do you want three years from now?' Most people can't say what they want three weeks from now."

And the same goes for Millennials, especially when they don't consider a car to be a necessity right now. But

Ford had a few clever ideas up its sleeve that managed to capture the attention of these young consumers.

Ford successfully launched one of the car industry's hottest Facebook apps—the Ford Mustang Customizer—which allows its millions of eager players the chance to trick out their dream Mustang in competition with their fellow car enthusiasts.

"If you look at numbers on social media, it's dominated by Millennials," says Connelly. "So although it's not just for Millennials, they are a huge driver of the success of our Facebook app."

Another example: In 2007, Ford partnered with Microsoft to launch SYNC, an integrated entertainment system. The Bluetooth-enabled technology connects the car to a cell phone, allowing the driver to make phone calls, play MP3 files, and operate the car's radio, navigation, and climate controls through voice commands, so the driver's eyes are always on the road. In addition to offering the connectivity that Millennials crave, SYNC was first rolled out in Ford's lower-priced Focus model, which Millennials were more likely to be able to afford.

Impact: With more than three million SYNC systems on the road today, the technology was a hit with Millennials, says Connelly. Not only was it initially offered in a lower-priced vehicle, leading to more purchases and goodwill among members of the generation, it also allows them to stay constantly

connected—something they value,
as covered earlier in this book.

"We think that's been one of our most successful ways of capturing the Millennials' attention because they are all about constant connectivity," says Connelly.

"We also wanted to democratize this technology by offering it in our lower-priced vehicle," she says. "Because of our success, it was launched throughout our entire portfolio."

Certainly, Ford took a huge risk in designing a car to meet the specific needs of Millennial consumers. (After all, just because you build it, that doesn't mean they will come.) But Ford correctly realized that the greater risk was complacency. So the carmaker got to know and understand the needs of a huge group of consumers—their future customers.

Rewards Work

Given that Millennials place such a high degree of importance on being a success in life, achieving status in a rewards program is also extremely desirable for them. No surprise, they tend to align their shopping loyalty with brands that offer rewards programs. According to Aimia's "Born This Way: The U.S. Millennial Loyalty Survey," Millennials are more likely than other generations to take part in customer loyalty programs, especially when there is a giveaway offered.[15] While Millennials "lag slightly behind other generations in participation in consumer loyalty programs, [. . .] when a reward or giveaway is involved, Millennial participation jumps to the front of the pack," according to a blog post that referenced the survey.[16] In fact, Millennials rate loyalty rewards as *the top incentive* they look for in exchange for sharing personal information with marketers.

And that's not all. The same survey found they are much more likely to tell their peers about the program, with Millennials being 50 percent more likely than other generations to say they would use social media like Facebook and Twitter to promote the programs they participated in.[17] This is a salient point for brands, given that Millennials have a strong influence on their peers.

What are Millennials looking for in a rewards program? If you've read the previous chapters in this book, you may be able to guess the three characteristics that ranked well above the others: free, fast, and easy. "Participation in the program should be free, rewards should come quickly, and signing up needs to be one-click easy," according to the "Born This Way" survey.[18]

We'd like to add one more rule: Don't take the rewards away. The next example explains why.

Online fashion retailer and flash-sale specialist RueLaLa, a members-only site, has garnered some Millennial love for its rewards program. With more than 5 million customers who visit the site frequently each month, the company is on a roll—and it attributes much of its success to its special loyalty programs. In one incarnation, a program specifically catered to the site's biggest diehards, offering them "a dedicated customer service number whose staff was charged with doing whatever it took to make the customers happy."[19] Like its competitor Gilt, RueLaLa deploys several Millennial marketing best practices when it comes to its rewards programs such as rewarding members with dollars for inviting friends. But what distinguishes it from its competitors?

According to one Millennial we surveyed, "Your dollars from inviting your friends never ever expire." Sounds like a no-brainer to us. Why reward your best advocates and supporters with a gift only to take it away from them later? That's the quickest way to lose a good friend!

For a slightly different take on the rewards model, consider fashion brand Lilly Pulitzer. In its quest to reach sorority women with its branded sorority collections, the company launched its campus representative recruitment program in 2012 targeted at Lilly Pulitzer–loving sorority members with strong campus connections. In exchange for promoting Lilly Pulitzer products to Greek chapters across the country, the company provides its campus reps with a host of perks, including a welcome package featuring items from its sorority collection, a $200 Lilly Pulitzer gift card at the end of the program, opportunities to earn more throughout the year, and the ability to provide input to the merchandising team for the creation of new sorority products. Who better to represent the brand to sororities on campus than women who live and breathe Greek life—and who love Lilly Pulitzer?

This effort follows the company's equally savvy strategy of launching a Facebook contest to crowdsource ideas for its sorority collections, build excitement for future product releases, and help beat the competition. As one of our Millennial survey respondents described it: "Vera Bradley used to be the quintessential sorority brand, but lost out big time [to Lilly Pulitzer]. Lilly not only engaged fans on Facebook with the campaign, but encouraged them to invite their friends to their first sorority-bag launch."

By recognizing and putting your best brand advocates on a pedestal for their support, you, too, will reap rewards.

Coupons Are King

In addition to upping the fun factor and rewarding them for their support, brands also need to be willing to engage with Millennial consumers in a helpful and friendly manner to build brand loyalty. What better way to do that than by offering exclusive deals and discounts via your company's social media channels?

This leads us back to Courtney's experiences. Although she uses Twitter mainly to keep up with her favorite celebrities, she does follow a few brands, especially ones that offer promotions that she can use. "I only really follow brands on Twitter that offer deals or discounts off on their products or services. And I love taking advantage of the discounts that many local restaurants offer," says Courtney. "Big brands don't typically do this."

If your brand isn't yet offering exclusive deals and discounts to these consumers through social media channels that have successfully broken down the communications barriers of yesteryear, there is a growing body of evidence suggesting that you should. A 2012 MPA and GfK MRI study on social media habits among 18- to 34-year olds found that Millennials are receptive to advertisers in general, especially when discounts via social media are involved. Indeed, 59 percent enter contests on Facebook or Twitter in order to win products or receive discounts, 53 percent download coupons from a company's Facebook page, and 51 percent redeem an offer from a company's Twitter feed or Facebook page. One out of three respondents said they visit or would visit a magazine's Facebook page for special offers from advertisers or the magazine.[20]

While the study was intended to highlight trends that magazine publishers need to be aware of when working with their advertising partners to implement programs of interest to this target audience, these findings prove salient to any company seeking to build a relationship with Millennial consumers like Courtney. The key takeaway here? Brands that take the opportunity to engage with Millennials in this way are the ones that will stand out.

Excellent Customer Service Matters, Too

While providing exclusive deals and promotions is a proven strategy for reaching Millennials, brands should also aim to be truly helpful in their interactions with these consumers through memorable customer service moments.

From our research we learned that, when shopping, Millennials like to receive help and approval from fashion consultants rather than just basic assistance. Female and male Millennial shoppers alike appreciate style-savvy fashion consultants who wear the store's merchandise in unique and creative ways that inspire fashion ideas.

Why does this matter? According to a survey by American Express, customers are willing to reward companies for top-notch service, spending 21 percent more with those that provide it![21] And thanks to the Millennial consumers' larger online social networks, companies that provide excellent customer service reap huge rewards when a happy Millennial consumer shares one of these memorable moments with his or her friends and associates via Facebook or Twitter.

Social media also make it easier for companies to go the extra mile to provide great service.

For instance, Best Buy's Twelpforce initiative provides customer support through Twitter. The service allows customers to tweet at the Twelpforce account for answers to questions ranging from a product's availability to its technical functions.

With more than 46,000 followers, Best Buy strives to create a functional listening strategy that allows the team to provide fast and efficient service to customers. Twelpforce, launched on a social media platform popular among Millennials, rates high with these consumers, who love to create online conversations with brands and who put a premium on instant gratification. It's a win-win: The customer receives needed support and feels personally cared for by the brand, while Best Buy provides its customers with a unique and effective participation strategy.[22]

"What's so great about social media is that it cuts out the middle man," says Joe Cox, Barkley's social media director, whom you met in Chapter 4. "Consumers can reach right out to let a brand know when something went wrong or even *when something went right*. Brands can generate a ton of goodwill among consumers by doing the littlest thing, like simply responding to a tweet because it's unexpected."

Another example is clothing retailer Zappos. Its entire core brand idea is focused on providing excellent customer service. Zappos operates on the premise of delivering "WOW" to all customers through 10 core values that drive brand operations such as working well with others and creating clear lines of communication.[23] Many of the Zappos' tenets hit on the very same values our study uncovered as being important to Millennials.

The brand facilitates conversation with its customers through Twitter, allowing for an atmosphere where customers feel they can contribute insights about Zappos products and, more important, be able to highlight customer service issue areas that need to be addressed.

"Before Zappos, I used to be the type of person who had to try on shoes before I bought them, but thanks to Zappos' excellent customer service, I've changed my ways. Now I shop online for shoes all of the time," said Caroline, a Millennial you first met in Chapter 5. "I was having trouble purchasing a pair of shoes one time, so I tweeted a question to the Zappos customer service account. It wasn't a big issue, but they gave me free shipping anyway for the inconvenience. Zappos is proof that you can really buy people's love!"

It should come as no surprise that Zappos scores high marks among Millennials like Caroline who say they prefer brands that value their input *and* strive to keep their customers happy. It's not simply about providing good deals, although that can help. As a LuxuryInstitute.com article states, "It is crucial for social media to be treated as a service channel in addition to a promotional channel. The installation of an uninformed employee, armed with no more than a hyperlink to a customer service page is only slightly better than ignoring comments made within social networks."[24] We couldn't have said it better ourselves.

Amazon is another company that excels in delivering a unique brand experience through the ability to compare competitive pricing, excellent customer service, automatic product suggestions, and easy returns. In-store retailers simply can't keep up.[25] Talk about a way to differentiate your brand and keep your customers loyal! Brick-and-mortar stores are becoming "data deserts," where consumers are unable to receive the level of in-depth information they crave.[26] In Interbrand's "Best Retail Brands 2012," Amazon ranked number 9 and cited "customer-centricity at the core of its brand strength."[27]

Take Their Feedback to Heart

To build loyalty among Millennial consumers, be a standout among your competitors by being the first to engage with consumers and act on their feedback and insights. But you'd better get started soon. According to Barkley's Joe Cox, brands have about three more years before this kind of interaction becomes expected and will no longer score you brownie points. Already, consumers are beginning to question the motives of companies that collect customer opinions. Indeed, about the same amount of Boomers (73 percent) and Millennials (71 percent) believe that companies care about customer opinions only because they intend to use them to influence how other consumers will view the brand, not because they care what their customers think, according to Bazaarvoice. However, despite believing that companies don't care about their opinions, Millennials still want to communicate with them and feel more strongly than Boomers (64 percent vs. 53 percent) that companies should offer more ways to share their opinions online.[28]

In addition to responding directly to customers' input by answering their questions and engaging with them on social media, prove that you care by taking action on their insights. Not only will it show that you are listening, it can also help enhance your product or service offering and improve customer relations. And don't hesitate to let customers know you've taken action because, according to Bazaarvoice, "When they know you care, they'll come back with more feedback, and these conversations create a valuable loyalty cycle."[29]

Brands That Care

When it comes to building loyalty among Millennial consumers, one additional item for your tool kit is the ability to tap into their desire to make a difference in the world.

You don't have to look far to find a study that highlights just how much this generation wants to make a positive impact. According to our survey, Millennials aren't volunteering any more community-service hours than their parents did. But they are certainly expressing an overwhelming interest in making a difference *and* supporting companies that do the same. Indeed, our findings underscore just how much this generation's purchase decisions are influenced by their opinions of a company's cause-marketing initiatives, with almost half of Millennial respondents saying they're more likely to buy a brand they know supports a cause.

In light of the Millennials' growing interest in supporting brands that give back, new companies like TOMS Shoes and FEED Projects—which helps provide meals to hungry children through every purchase of a FEED-branded product through the company's partnership with the United Nations World Food Programme—are thriving among Millennial consumers.

"We've been able to provide 60 million school meals to hungry children worldwide, while 46,000 kids in America have been directly impacted by our efforts," says FEED Projects Millennial-age cofounder and CEO, Lauren Bush (who also happens to be President George H.W. Bush's granddaughter). "Our success is measured by how many kids get fed."

For brand managers who are searching for ways to engage Millennial consumers, it's critical to show that you are a brand that cares. But proceed with caution. As we've said before, these savvy consumers have a good nose for phoniness. They know when you're merely supporting a cause to sell your product. Pink and green labels alone won't get you far with these consumers. "It's not about slapping a ribbon on a product any longer," said Carol Cone, executive vice president and cause-marketing expert at Edelman, in a story Christie wrote for *USA Today* in 2011. They do want "deeper involvement in social issues and expect brands and companies to provide various means of engagement." What the most successful companies have in common "is an overarching message and purpose, and they're making it transparent."[30]

For companies that do get it right with Millennials, the upside is big. Thirty-seven percent of Millennials say they are willing to purchase a product or service to support a cause they believe in, even if it means paying a bit more.

Cause campaigns that are currently winning with this generation include legacy campaigns such as Yoplait's Save Lids to Save Lives with partner Susan G. Komen for the Cure (breast cancer) and a youth-oriented campaign by Gap with partner Product (RED), fighting AIDS in Africa, which scored much higher among Millennials than non-Millennials in terms of awareness, according to our recent research. See Figure 7-2.

These campaigns succeed because they have partnered with established, well-respected charities. Given this trust, Millennials believe they can contribute to causes they care about more easily through these companies' programs than through their own initiative. They also value charitable contributions through cause marketing because of the ease of participation and the scope of the impact that a corporate-based charitable program can have in comparison to an individual donation.

Established cause programs are top of mind
Fashion and beauty brands resonate with Millennials

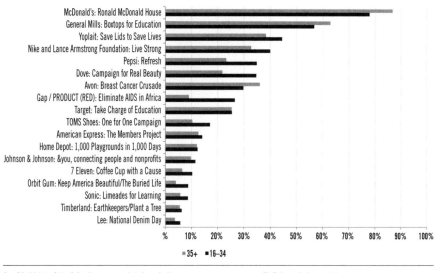

Q – C3: Which of the following cause-related marketing programs are you aware of? (Select all that apply)
N – 16–34 yr olds – 4,259; 35+ yr olds – 1,234

Source: Barkley, The Boston Consulting Group, and Service Management Group, "American Millennials: Deciphering the Enigma Generation," September 2011.

Figure 7-2 Cause programs important to Millennials.

"The success of companies like [FEED Projects] serve as a call to action to companies that it's more than just the bottom line," says Lauren Bush. "It's a shift in what values matter most. It's not just about making money; it's about making the world a better place. I think consumers, especially young ones, are demanding that from companies today."

Summing up, an affiliation with a cause is more important to the Millennial generation than to any previous generation. For a brand that is searching for ways to engage and tap into this next generation of consumers, showing them that you care is critical, but you must do so authentically.

"Don't just talk the talk. Companies need to walk the walk," Bush says.

When it comes to building loyalty with consumers who are *not* inclined toward loyalty, the overall goal should be to "create an emotional connection with this group—a proven method of driving purchase behavior among Millennials."[31]

Do this through innovative products, packaging, and promotional programs that reflect this generation's quest to look like they're living well for less. Establish and grow loyalty among Millennial shoppers with a value proposition firmly founded on their rituals, needs, and wants. And play this out by prominently reflecting the value proposition across marketing programs and platforms.

CHAPTER 7: KEY TAKEAWAYS

▸ **Price is the most important factor when it comes to Millennials' purchase decisions.** It also dictates where they shop. Brands need to consider their affinity for a good deal when developing their marketing plans for a new product or service.

▸ **The economic downturn has impacted the Millennial generation's willingness to be loyal to a brand.** While brand loyalty may not count for much among Millennial consumers these days, brands can win easy brownie points—and loyalty—by engaging with Millennial consumers in a fun and real way.

▸ **Millennials need a reason to choose your brand.** Brands need to focus on value. Ask yourself what differentiates your brand from another? Why should a Millennial choose you over your competitor? Show Millennials your assets, and demonstrate why they should choose you.

▸ **Customer service ranks high with Millennials.** Brands that show Millennials how much they value their business are finding increasing success. At a time when brand loyalty can be difficult to maintain, this can be a way to secure Millennial loyalty. Brands should make loyalty part of their brand identity.

▸ **Millennials want to make a positive impact on the world, and they express a willingness to shop with companies that do the same.** Win over these bighearted consumers by supporting a cause that has a relevant connection to your brand.

CHAPTER 8

Epilogue

Now that you are familiar with the new rules of Marketing to Millennials and you have a better understanding of the generation, you likely have some big questions, such as: *Where do I start?*

Millennials are not a homogeneous cohort, and applying the new rules is not a one-size-fits-all solution. Each rule can be interpreted differently to optimize the targeting of your core audience.

Before closing, we thought it would be helpful to leave you with some additional considerations and suggestions as you move forward with your own plans for engaging members of the exciting Millennial generation.

Keep Up with Technology Trends

Technology fuels Millennial culture, as members of this generation are quick to embrace emerging digital, social, and mobile technology. Consequently, Millennial culture generates entrepreneurs who create new social and mobile tools. This means it's critical to stay abreast of what's next in both technology and Millennial culture. After all, they're related. And the emerging trends will likely both enable and impact consumer behavior.

To keep up with these developments, subscribe to cultural and tech-trend sharing websites such as Trend Hunter, Iconoculture, Mashable, BuzzFeed, and PSFK. These sites have thousands of active participants who stay on top of what's new and share tips online.

Within your own organization, consider creating a content-sharing platform to capture and distribute ideas on Millennials and emerging trends. Your company likely has several Millennial-age employees who would be eager to share their insights. It would be wise to tap into an already built-in audience within your organization.

Last but not least, content-sharing social tools such as Pinterest can help gather and organize articles on Millennial consumer trends. Such sites are also inundated by Millennial users, offering the opportunity to gain insights from and communicate with this generation.

Engage Millennials in Everything You Do

As we have pointed out time and time again, Millennials are active participants, not passive consumers. When developing a strategy that will effectively engage these consumers, consider using a 2 × 2 matrix such as the one in Figure 8-1 to evaluate your brand potential and ideas.

On the x-axis of the matrix, "Participation" measures the degree to which consumers are actively engaged in the brand. On the y-axis, "Shareworthy" evaluates how much the core brand idea enables consumers to share with peers.

There are three phases of participation: (1) cocreate the product or service itself, (2) cocreate the customer journey, and (3) cocreate marketing, not limited to social media.

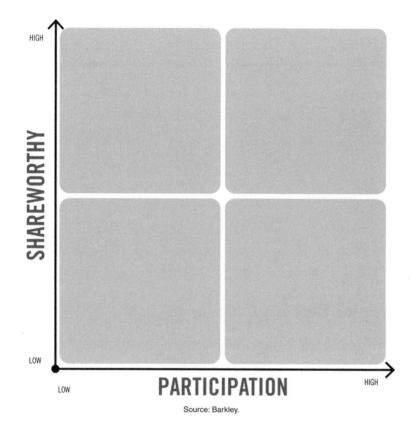

Source: Barkley.

Figure 8-1 A matrix of participation and shareworthiness.

There are two common roads to shareworthy ideas: purpose and disruption. If your idea has both a purpose and is disruptive—causing people to stop what they're doing, pay attention, and engage with your brand—then you've reached a high-high on the matrix. At the end of the day, shareworthy is directly related to both peer affirmation and understanding that Millennials share because it makes them feel better about themselves. It's not all about your brand.

When you apply the matrix to your brand's activities, ask yourself the following questions: Are you working on a shareworthy idea? Have you enabled opportunities for Millennial participation? Can you set up a framework for seeking Millennial input on your products or services, customer journey, and marketing efforts? Brands that can successfully engage Millennials will rank high in both shareworthiness and participation.

Ultimately, Millennials want to participate in all phases of product development. By not only considering their input but taking the extra step of building your functional and emotional brand benefits around it, you add a catalytic agent to your marketing. Similarly, if your brand has an undeniable shareworthy quality to it, it becomes increasingly enticing for Millennials.

Strive for Content Excellence

In the past, great brands tended to focus on being "creatively excellent." A brand could do so by producing strong design and copy. While still important, creative excellence should no longer be a brand's overarching goal. Instead, it exists as an important subset of the larger opportunity that is "content excellence," as illustrated in Figure 8-2.

A brand that focuses on content excellence is dedicated to creating ideas that are shareworthy in all areas. A brand that dis-

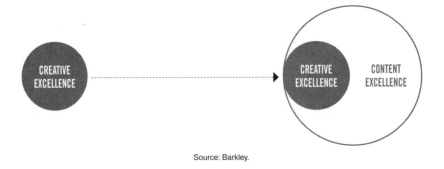

Source: Barkley.

Figure 8-2 Progression from creative excellence to content excellence.

plays content excellence targets consumers through all channels. Each idea that emerges from a content-excellent brand embodies and conveys the company's core brand idea.

Content excellence ensures consistency across all platforms. A brand will no longer simply seek to create a successful one-off creative TV spot but will aim for a fully integrated campaign. Creative excellence is important, but it's only a part of content excellence.

So why strive to make the transition with your brand from creative excellence to content excellence? Simply put, Millennials value brands that focus on the latter. They value consistent messaging and appreciate being invited into the conversation about a brand. Millennials have a desire to share with others and gravitate toward brands that allow them to do so. Millennials love a good advertisement, but even more, they appreciate having access to a platform to talk about and share it.

Good Content Is Key

As social creatures, Millennials seek interaction with their favorite brands. And social interaction requires interesting content that will grab the attention of the Millennial generation. The task of creating that content is up to the company or brand.

Do you have a content curator on your team who can help channel and facilitate these interactions? You may consider adding the role of chief content officer to your team, a person who keeps all content throughout the company on the same set of higher business objectives, ensuring consistency of the brand's voice across all channels.

As we discussed in Chapter 4, companies are beginning to recognize content as a highly valuable business asset. Though not yet fully embraced, companies are recognizing the ability of content to differentiate their brands at a time when almost everything else has been commoditized. Companies are searching for ways to stand out to their target audiences. And nothing stands out like content.

If appointing a chief content officer isn't feasible (given budgetary constraints, for instance), consider identifying an individual within the company who has not only the requisite knowledge but the authority and backing of the C-suite as well. If you approach content creation correctly, the impact of this role should reach across all aspects of your business.

In the "Age of the Customer,"[1] a time when the customer matters more than any other strategic imperative, empowered buyers demand a new level of brand experience. At the forefront of this movement are Millennials. They are social creatures who expect their brands to engage them. If that expectation isn't met, they'll leave and spend their money elsewhere. Figure 8-3 from

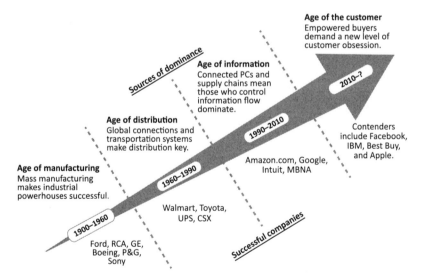

Source: Age of the Customer—Source Forrester Research 10/2011 "Why Customer Experience? Why Now?"

Figure 8-3: Forrester's depiction of the progression to the
Age of the Customer.

Forrester Research, Inc., describes this evolution to the current "Age of the Customer."

When planning content management, be sure to address and identify the processes, tools, and resources required to launch and maintain ongoing quality of the brand message. You must determine how those decisions are made and who has ownership of the decisions (as well as their effects).

No Brand Can Afford to Ignore Millennials

While your brand's core target audience today may be older, Millennials are a generation that cannot be ignored. Though they may seem far off from your target audience now, they will eventually transition into your core demographic. It's better to get to know and engage them early on, building their loyalty over time.

So how do you get started? Consider using some form of this investment model, as shown in Figure 8-4.

Hypothetically, to get this right, focus 75 percent of your funds on your core consumers of today with strategies that address their needs. Another 20 percent of your funds can be spent on emerging opportunities, and 5 percent on "blue ocean" opportunities that exist in an unknown market space.

We recommend some split in your budget to ensure that the team responsible for brand stewardship maintains a healthy focus on what's driving the business today without ignoring "what's next." Keep in mind, if you don't have any efforts in emerging and blue ocean opportunities, you are giving your competitors the chance to use disruption strategies to grab your customers and kill your business.

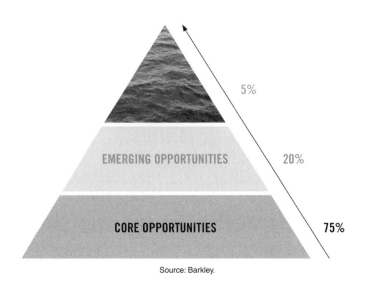

Source: Barkley.

Figure 8-4 A suggested investment model.

Another tactic you can use in resource allocation is to identify a Millennial-centric approach and see if your core target audience will embrace it as well. Many brands have older customers who are open to and influenced by what Millennials think. So don't assume your older core audience won't be enticed by the same marketing measures. We should also point out here that Millennials are the first generation to actively try to encourage older generations to adopt their habits and beliefs. Can you find common threads of interest between today's older core consumers and tomorrow's Millennials? If so, you may have identified a great way for a brand that's preferred by older consumers to leverage its budget without losing its base.

For example, the 127-year-old brand, Ball® home canning brand, which we showcased in a case study in Chapter 5, traditionally has an older core target audience. Despite this, Jarden Home Brands realized it didn't want to neglect younger generations of enthusiastic canners and potential customers. The Ball®

home canning brand appealed to new canners through an integrated campaign that ran on television, on social media, and in print ads. Jarden Home Brands positioned the Ball® home canning brand as a support system for new canners, promising to be there every step of the way. The Ball® home canning website was updated with recipes and useful content, increasing its Millennial allure.

Likewise, through a strong presence on its Facebook page, the number of fans grew from 5,000 to more than 59,000 over the course of the campaign. On arguably the most popular Millennial social media platform, such an impressive showing undoubtedly helped the brand appeal to its newly added target audience.

These considerations should set any company out there on the path for successful implementation of a more robust business that will not only maintain healthy ties to its current customers but also allow for engagement with a generation that no brand can afford to ignore.

Notes

Chapter 1: Who Are They?

1. Bill George, "Brands Are Dead. Welcome to the Participation Economy," October 6, 2009, http://www.billgeorge.org/page/kevin-roberts-brands-are-dead--welcome-to-the-participation-economy.

2. "Android Open Source Project," Google, http://source.android.com/about/philosophy.html.

3. "iOS," February 22, 2013, http://en.wikipedia.org/wiki/IOS.

4. Simon Sage, "iOS Slammed as 'Crystal Prison' by Electronic Frontier Foundation," iMore, May 30, 2012, http://www.imore.com/ios-slammed-crystal-prison-electronic-frontier-foundation.

5. Micah Lee and Peter Eckersley, "Apple's Crystal Prison and the Future of Open Platforms," Electronic Frontier Foundation, May 29, 2012, https://www.eff.org/deeplinks/2012/05/apples-crystal-prison-and-future-open-platforms.

6. Sage, "iOS Slammed."

7. "IDC: Android Jumps to 68.1% Global Market Share, iOS Slips to 16.9%," Android Authority, August 8, 2012, http://www.androidauthority.com/idc-android-jumps-to-68-1-global-market-share-ios-slips-16-9-106446/.

8. Krush website, http://www.krush.com/.

9. "Gender Shift: Are Women the New Men?," Havas Worldwide, *Prosumer Report*, 2010, p. 7, http://www.prosumer-report.com/gender/wp-content/uploads/2011/04/GenderShift_final72.pdf.

10. "New Study on Millennials' Social Media Habits Shows Content Isn't Always King," The Economist Group, September 7, 2012,

http://www.economistgroup.com/leanback/lean-back-reading/new-study-on-millenials/.

11. Lisa B. Kahn, "The Long-Term Labor Market Consequences of Graduating from College in a Bad Economy," Yale School of Management, August 13, 2009 (forthcoming in *Labour Economics*), cited in *Millennials: Confident. Connected. Open to Change*, Pew Research Center, 2010, http://www.pewsocialtrends.org/2010/02/24/millennials-confident-connected-open-to-change/.

12. *Millennials: Confident. Connected. Open to Change*, Pew Research Center 2010, http://www.pewsocialtrends.org/2010/02/24/millennials-confident-connected-open-to-change/ (accessed on June 1, 2012).

13. Larissa Faw, "Why Millennials Are Spending More Than They Earn, and Parents Are Footing the Bill," *Forbes*, May 18, 2012, http://www.forbes.com/sites/larissafaw/2012/05/18/why-millennials-are-spending-more-than-they-earn/.

14. "American Express Business Insights Data Show Full-Price Online Luxury Fashion Spending Sizzling as New York Fashion Week Heats Up," American Express, February 10, 2012, http://about.americanexpress.com/news/pr/2012/nyfw.aspx).

15. Faw, "Why Millennials Are Spending More."

16. "American Express Publishing and Harrison Group Announce 2012 Trend Data from the Annual Survey of Affluence and Wealth in America; Results Show Luxury Spending Focused on Worth and Quality in Life," American Express Publishing, May 9, 2012, http://www.amexpub.com/downloads/2012-05-09_AEP_Harris.pdf.

17. Faw, "Why Millennials Are Spending More."

18. Larissa Faw, "Meet The Millennial 1%: Young, Rich, And Redefining Luxury," October 2, 2012, http://www.forbes.com/sites/larissafaw/2012/10/02/meet-the-millennial-1-young-rich-and-redefining-luxury/.

19. Ibid.

20. "Survey: 85% of New College Grads Move Back in with Mom and Dad," Time NewsFeed, May 10, 2011, http://newsfeed.time .com/2011/05/10/survey-85-of-new-college-grads-moving-back -in-with-mom-and-dad/#ixzz1eHp2H0YH.

21. *The Millennials: A Portrait of Generation Next*, Pew Research Center, 2010, http://pewsocialtrends.org/files/2010/10/millennials -confident-connected-open-to-change.pdf.

Chapter 2: The New Rules of Marketing to Millennials

1. "Millennials: The Challenger Generation," Havas Worldwide, *Prosumer Report*, Vol 11, 2011, pg. 3. http://www.prosumer-report .com/blog/?page_id=8692.

2. "Ethnography," *Wikipedia*, last modified June 2012, http://en .wikipedia.org/wiki/Ethnography.

3. "Macy's, Inc. Outlines Enhanced Focus to Drive Growth Among Millennial Customers," BusinessWire, March 21, 2012, http:// www.businesswire.com/news/home/20120321005258/en/ Macy's-Outlines-Enhanced-Focus-Drive-Growth-Millennial.

4. Alec Levenson, "Making Sense of the Millennial Generation: What Organizations Need to Know," University of Southern California, Center for Effective Organizations, http://ceo.usc.edu/ news/making_sense_of_the_millennial_1.html.

5. Christine Barton, Jeff Fromm, and Chris Egan, "The Millennial Consumer: Debunking Stereotypes, bcgperspectives.com, April 16, 2012,https://www.bcgperspectives.com/content/articles/consumer _insight_marketing_millennial_consumer/.

6. "Gender Shift: Are Women the New Men?," Havas Worldwide, *Prosumer Report*, 2010, p. 7, http://www.prosumer-report.com/ gender/wp-content/uploads/2011/04/GenderShift_final72.pdf.

7. "Jobs and Economic Security for America's Women," report from the U.S. National Economic Council, October 2010.

8. "Gender Shift," Havas Worldwide, *Prosumer Report.*

9. "Women Call the Shots at Home; Public Mixed on Gender Roles in Jobs," Pew Research Social and Demographic Trends, September 25, 2008, http://pewresearch.org/pubs/967/gender-power.

10. "Gender Shift," Havas Worldwide, *Prosumer Report.*

Chapter 3: Engage These Early Adopters of New Technologies

1. Cara Fuggetta, "New Zuberance Product: Employee Advocacy Solution," ZuberRants, August 9, 2012, http://blog.zuberance.com/product/new-zuberance-product-employee-advocacy-solution/.

2. Annie Pilon, "Zuberance Turns Employees into Brand Advocates," Small Business Trends, August 17, 2012, http://smallbiztrends.com/2012/08/zuberance-turns-employees-into-brand-advocates.html.

3. Laura B. Weiss, "Study Predicts Always-On Generation Will Excel at Multitasking; Lag in Patience and Focus," The Digital Shift, February 29, 2012, http://www.thedigitalshift.com/2012/02/research/study-predicts-always-on-generation-will-excel-at-multitasking-lag-in-patience-and-focus/.

4. John Jannarone, "Forecast for Best Buy: Worst Is Yet to Come," Heard on the Street, *The Wall Street Journal* (online), March 4, 2011, http://online.wsj.com/article/SB10001424052748703300904576178740814079726.html.

5. George Anderson, "Retailers Fear Becoming Amazon's 'Showroom'," *Forbes,* July 14, 2011, http://www.forbes.com/sites/retailwire/2011/07/14/retailers-fear-becoming-amazons-showroom/.

6. Christine Barton, Lara Koslow, Jeff Fromm, and Chris Egan, "Millennial Passions: Food, Fashion and Friends," bcgperspectives .com, November 6, 2012, https://www.bcgperspectives.com/ content/articles/consumer_insight_consumer_products_millennial _passions/.

7. Dave Haynes, "Nike Raises Bar for Digital Retail in New London Pop-up Store," Sixteen Nine, March 15, 2012, http:// sixteen-nine.net/2012/03/15/nike-raises-bar-for-digital-retail-in -new-london-pop-up-store/.

8. Gardiner Morse and Ron Johnson, "Retail Isn't Broken. Stores Are: An Interview with Ron Johnson," *Harvard Business Review,* December 2011, http://hbr.org/2011/12/retail-isnt-broken-stores -are/.

9. Lydia Dishman, "Sephora's Smart Social and Digital Makeover," *Forbes,* April 9, 2012, http://www.forbes.com/sites/lydiadishman/ 2012/04/09/sephoras-smart-social-and-digital-makeover/.

Chapter 4: Build a Listening and Participation Strategy

1. Center for New Media Research, *The Millennials in the Adult World,* August 1, 2012, http://www.mediapost.com/publications/ article/179908/the-millennials-in-the-adult-world.html?utm _source=feedburner&utm_medium=feed&utm_campaign =Feedpercent3A+research-brief+(MediaPost+percent7C +Research+Brief).

2. "Millennial Shopper: Tapping Into the Next Growth Segment," SymphonyIRI Group Consumer Network report, June/July 2012.

3. Julianne Pepitone, "Why Cable Is Going to Cost You Even More," CNNMoney.com, January 9, 2010, http://money.cnn.com /2010/01/06/news/companies/cable_bill_cost_increase/.

4. Derek Thompson and Jordan Weissmann, "The Cheapest Generation: Why Millennials Aren't Buying Cars or Houses, and What That Means for the Economy," *The Atlantic,* September 2012.

5. "Understanding the Intricate Digital Behaviors of Young Consumers," Forrester Research, Inc., March 1, 2011.

6. Ibid.

7. Ibid.

8. Jacqueline Anderson, former Forrester Research analyst, as quoted in "Young Users Hating on Brands," *AdWeek,* March 9, 2011, http://www.adweek.com/news/technology/young-users-hating-brands-125949.

9. "Peter Shankman Tweet Joke Leads to Morton's Surprise Steak Dinner at Newark Airport," tweets first posted August 18, 2011, updated October 18, 2011, http://www.huffingtonpost.com/2011/08/18/peter-shankman-mortons-steak-tweet_n_930744.html.

10. Chris Horton, "5 Ways Pepsi's Use of Social Media Is Right On," SocialMedia Today, May 17, 2012, http://socialmediatoday.com/synecoretech/509355/5-ways-pepsis-use-social-media-right.

11. Michele Linn, "Joe Pulizzi on Content Marketing: Content Is the Essence of Marketing," Conversionation, September 14, 2011, http://www.conversionation.net/2011/09/joe-pulizzi-on-content-marketing-content-is-the-essence-of-marketing/.

12. Ibid.

13. The Nielsen Company, "Global Trust in Advertising and Brand Messages," report, April 2012, http://www.fi.nielsen.com/site/documents/NielsenTrustinAdvertisingGlobalReportApril2012.pdf.

14. Joe Pulizzi, "Coca-Cola Bets the Farm on Content Marketing: Content 2020," Content Marketing Institute, January 4, 2012, http://blog.junta42.com/2012/01/coca-cola-content-marketing-20-20/.

15. "Coca-Cola Content 2020 Part One," TheCognitiveMedia, uploaded to YouTube, August 10, 2011, http://www.youtube.com/watch?feature=player_embedded&v=LerdMmWjU_E.

16. Stephanie Tilton, "Coca-Cola's Content Strategy: 3 Lessons for B2B Marketers," Content Marketing Institute, February 15, 2012, http://www.contentmarketinginstitute.com/2012/02/coca-colas -content-strategy-lessons-for-marketers/.

17. Ibid.

18. Laura Stampler, "Behind-the-Scenes of an Epic Old Spice Commercial Shot in One Take," Business Insider, October 15, 2012, http://www.businessinsider.com/how-old-spice-shot-an-epic -commercial-in-one-take-2012-10.

19. Bill Mickey, "People StyleWatch Leverages Its Social Media Loyalists," Folio, August 14, 2012, http://www.foliomag.com/2012/ people-stylewatch-leverages-its-social-media-loyalists.

20. Ibid.

21. Ibid.

22. Ibid.

23. My Starbucks Idea website, Starbucks Corporation, http://my starbucksidea.force.com/.

24. "On a Bet, Party People Fill KLM Flight to Miami Using Twitter," Springwise.com, December 28, 2010, http://www.springwise .com/marketing_advertising/fly2miami/.

Chapter 5: Make Them Look Good Among Their Peers

1. "Talking to Strangers: Millennials Trust People over Brands," Bazaarvoice, January 2012, http://www.bazaarvoice.com/files/ whitepapers/BV_whitepaper_millennials.pdf.

2. Jack Loechner, "The Millennials in the Adult World," research brief from the Center for Media Research, MediaPost, August 1, 2012, http://www.mediapost.com/publications/article/179908/the -millennials-in-the-adult-world.html?utm_source=feedburner

&utm_medium=feed&utm_campaign=Feedpercent3A+research
-brief+(MediaPost+percent7C+Research+Brief).

3. "Talking to Strangers," Bazaarvoice, January 2012.

4. Ibid.

5. SymphonyIRIGroup, "Millennials' Sentiments Show Greater
Volatility Than Those of Other Age Groups, Resulting in Contin-
ued Frugal Practices; New Media Is Strong Influence on Purchase
Behaviors," July 11, 2012, http://www.symphonyiri.com/portals/
0/articlePdfs/T_Tpercent20Junepercent202012percent20
Millenialpercent20Shoppers.pdf.

6. Disclosure: Jarden Home Brands is a Barkley client.

7. *Ball* and Ball® TMs Ball Corporation, used under license to
Hearthmark LLC d/b/a Jarden Home Brands. Ball Corporation is
not associated with Jarden Home Brands.

8. Diana Ransom, "Product Placement's Future: The 'Gossip Girl,'
Birchbox Mashup?," *Young Entrepreneur,* April 17, 2012, www
.google.com/url?sa &rct=j&q=&esrc=s&source=web&cd=2&ved
=0CEYQFjAB&url=http://www.youngentrepreneur.com/blog/
product-placements-future-the-gossip-girl-birchbox-mashup/
&ei=cVCdUJftKsf6yQGt2oGoAw&usg=AFQjCNHj0fck1L4E
MJpNoKmrsE-gkGiz2A&sig2=h_sfm0OrF5u-EWzFVs8—w.

9. The Futures Company, *Millennials in Crisis: What the Team
Dynamic and the Crisis of Chrysalis Mean for Marketers,* March 29,
2011.

10. Jenna Johnson, "Steve Jobs' Millennial Fan Club Is Devoted to
Apple, but Why?," Post Local, *Washington Post,* October 6, 2011,
http://www.washingtonpost.com/blogs/campus-overload/post/
why-are-many-millennials-so-dedicated-to-apple/2011/10/06/
gIQARwZNQL_blog.html.

11. Jean Twenge, Generation Me: Why Today's Young Americans
Are More Confident, Assertive, and Entitled—And More Miser-
able Than Ever Before (New York: Free Press, 2007).

12. "Foursquare Passes 20 Million Users," Ypulse, April 16, 2012, http://www.ypulse.com/post/view/ypulse-essentials-foursquare -passes-20-million-users-music-festivals-millen.

13. The Futures Company, *Millennials in Crisis.*

14. Ibid.

Chapter 6: Design a Sense of Fun and Adventure

1. Teresa Novellino, "Beauty Site Birchbox Gets a $10.5M Injection," UpstartBusinessJournal,August18,2011,http://upstart.bizjournals .com/money/loot/2011/08/18/subscription-ecommerce-site -birchbox-gets-10-million-in-funding.html?page=all.

2. Ibid.

3. Hadley Malcolm, "Personal Stylists Just a Click Away," *USA Today,* October 14, 2012, http://www.usatoday.com/story/money/ business/2012/10/14/online-shopping-personal-stylists/1580749.

4. Ibid.

5. Ibid.

6. "Losing the Courage of Your Disruption,"The Anti-Marketer, October 2, 2008, http://www.anti-marketer.com/disruptive_marketing/.

7. Emily Glazer, "A David and Gillette Story," *The Wall Street Journal,* April 12, 2012, http://online.wsj.com/article/SB10001424052 70230362400457733810378993413414.html.

8. Adam Tschorn, "Gillette Taps Benjamin, Brody and Bernal for ProGlide Styler Ads," All the Rage, *Los Angeles Times,* January 23, 2012, http://latimesblogs.latimes.com/alltherage/2012/01/gillette -taps-brody-benjamin-and-bernal-as-facial-hair-ambassadors .html.

9. "DollarShaveClub.com—Our Blades Are F***ing Great," You Tube, March 6, 2012, http://www.youtube.com/watch?v=ZUG9 qYTJMsI.

10. Bill Carter, "In the Tastes of Young Men, Humor Is Most Prized, a Survey Finds," *The New York Times,* February 19, 2012, http://www.nytimes.com/2012/02/20/business/media/comedy-central-survey-says-young-men-see-humor-as-essential.html?_r=0.

11. Ibid.

12. Ibid.

13. "About Movember," Movember and Sons, http://us.movember.com/about/.

14. Tony Merevick, "Movember Cofounder Talks Growing Men's Health Awareness, One 'Mo' at a Time," Chicago Phoenix, November 1, 2012, http://chicagophoenix.com/2012/11/01/movember-cofounder-talks-mens-health-awareness-one-mo-at-a-tim/.

15. Ellen Lee, "Millennial Entrepreneurs Bypass the Unemployment Line," *USA Today,* November 30, 2011, http://www.usatoday.com/money/smallbusiness/story/2011-12-03/cnbc-millennial-entrepreneurs/51513386/1, accessed June 1, 2012.

16. "Dispatches from the Millennial Mega Mashup: MTV's Nick Shore on 'Generation Innovation,'" Ypulse, May 11, 2012, http://www.ypulse.com/post/view/dispatches-from-the-millennial-mega-mashup-mtvs-nick-shore-on-generation-innovation.

17. Ibid.

18. Ibid.

19. "MTV Engages Its Viewers for Innovation; Need for Speed Is Met Using Its Private Community Fueled by Communispace," Communispace, http://www.communispace.com/mtv-engages-tv-viewers-case-study/.

Chapter 7: Don't Give Them a Reason to Cheat on You

1. "Millennial Shopper: Tapping Into the Next Growth Segment," SymphonyIRI Group Consumer Network report, June/July 2012.

2. Ibid.

3. Ibid.

4. Ibid.

5. Brad Tuttle, "I'll Trade You My Skinny Jeans for Your Skinny Jeans," *Time* Business & Money, May 7, 2012, http://business .time.com/2012/05/07/ill-trade-you-my-skinny-jeans-for-your -skinny-jeans/.

6. Sapna Maheshwari, "Apparel-Swapping Millennials Eschew Stores and Malls," Bloomberg, May 3, 2012, http://www.bloomberg .com/news/2012-05-03/apparel-swapping-millennials-eschew -stores-and-malls.html.

7. Ibid.

8. "Millennial Shopper," SymphonyIRI Consumer Network report.

9. Ibid.

10. Carlotta Mast, "What Are All Those Millennials Doing in Whole Foods?," New Hope 360.com, August 7, 2012, http://newhope360 .com/blog/what-are-all-those-millennials-doing-whole-foods.

11. Gardiner Morse and Ron Johnson, "Retail Isn't Broken. Stores Are: An Interview with Ron Johnson," *Harvard Business Review,* December 2011, http://hbr.org/2011/12/retail-isnt-broken-stores -are/.

12. Nick Bilton, "Disruptions: For Teenagers, a Car or a Smart-phone?," *New York Times* Bits, November 20, 2011, http://bits .blogs.nytimes.com/2011/11/20/a-teenage-question-a-car-or-a -smart-phone.

13. Ibid.

14. Ibid.

15. Rick Ferguson, "Born This Way: The U.S. Millennial Loyalty Survey: How Generation Y Will Reshape Customer Loyalty,

Aimia, 2011, http://www.aimia.com/files/doc_downloads/Aimia
_GenY_Nov9_US.pdf.

16. "Millennials to Loyalty Programs: Fast, Free and Easy," blog post, Generational Insights, October 13, 2011, http://www.generational insights.com/millennials-to-loyalty-programs-fast-free-and-easy/.

17. Ferguson, "Born This Way" survey.

18. Ibid.

19. Susan Nichols, "How Rue La La Creates the Ooh La La," Apparel, September 8, 2011, http://apparel.edgl.com/case-studies/How -Rue-La-La-Creates-the-Ooh-La-La-75431.

20. Emma Bazilian, "Millennials Engage with Magazines via Social Media, but They Want Something Out of It," *AdWeek*, August 23, 2012, http://www.adweek.com/news/press/study-millennials -engage-magazines-social media-143075.

21. Shea Bennett, "Social Media Users Spend 21% More on Brands That Exceed Customer Service Expectations," All Twitter, Media Bistro, May 3, 2012, http://www.mediabistro.com/alltwitter/ social-media-consumer-service_b22105.

22. Drew Neisser, "Twelpforce: Marketing That Isn't Marketing," *Fast Company*, May 17, 2010, http://www.fastcompany.com/1648739/ twelpforce-marketing-isn%E2%80%99t-marketing.

23. "Zappos Family Core Values," Zappos.com, http://about.zappos .com/our-unique-culture/zappos-core-values/embrace-and-drive -change.

24. Adam Broitman, "Six Ways to Serve Loyal Consumers in a Smartphone Age," Luxury Institute News, September 5, 2012, http://luxuryinstitute.com/blog/?tag=social-media.

25. Ashley Lutz, "Here's a Perfect Illustration of Why Amazon Will Beat Traditional Retailers," Business Insider, October 18, 2012, http://www.businessinsider.com/why-amazon-will-beat-other -retailers-2012-10.

26. Mark Hurst, "The Future of Retail, Reflected in a Skillet," Creative Good, October 17, 2012, http://creativegood.com/blog/the-future-of-retail/.

27. "Best Retail Brands 2012," Interbrand, http://www.interbrand.com/en/BestRetailBrands/2012-Best-Retail-Brands.aspx#page-wrap.

28. "Talking to Strangers: Millennials Trust People over Brands," Bazaarvoice, January 2012, http://www.bazaarvoice.com/files/whitepapers/BV_whitepaper_millennials.pdf.

29. Ibid.

30. Christie Garton, "Consumers Are Drawn to Products with a Charitable Connection," *USA Today*, July 18, 2011, http://yourlife.usatoday.com/mind-soul/doing-good/story/2011/07/consumers-are-drawn-to-products-with-a-charitable-connection/49467406/1.

31. "Millennial Shopper," SymphonyIRI Consumer Network report.

Chapter 8: Epilogue

1. Moira Dorsey, Kerry Bodine, with Allison Stone, "Why Customer Experience? Why Now?," Forrester Research Inc., October 4, 2011, http://www.forrester.com/Why+Customer+Experience+Why+Now/fulltext/-/E-RES60903?objectid=RES60903.

Index

About the Authors

Jeff Fromm is the executive vice president at Barkley, the largest 100 percent employee-owned advertising agency in the United States. In addition to his marketing degree from The Wharton School at the University of Pennsylvania, Jeff has more than 25 years of brand marketing experience. On behalf of Barkley, he spearheaded the Millennials research partnership with The Boston Consulting Group and Service Management Group. Jeff is the founder of Share.Like.Buy, a Millennial insights and marketing conference, and the lead editor of a blog, www.millennialmarketing.com.

Barkley believes that creativity and innovation can change the world. Fiercely independent, Barkley's goal is to help build the biggest future possible for its clients. Barkley provides fully integrated advertising and marketing services as well as specialized services through four partner companies: Crossroads, PR and cause marketing; Blacktop, branding and design; Barkley REI, interactive marketing; and Grenadier, strategic and creative. For more information, please visit http://barkleyus.com/.

Christie Garton left the legal field in 2006 to found her company, U Chic Media, which provides content, products, and resources targeted to the female college student audience. Since its founding, U Chic Media has helped thousands of Millennial women successfully navigate the college experience, primarily through its website at http://uchic.com/. Garton is also the author of the bestselling guide to college for women, *U Chic: The College Girl's Guide to Everything* (3rd edition, Sourcebooks, 2013) and *U Chic's Diploma Diaries: The Chic Grad's Guide to Work, Love and Everything in Between* (Sourcebooks, 2013).

Garton graduated magna cum laude from the University of Kansas with a double degree in business administration and French in 2001 and from the University of Pennsylvania Law School in 2006. A noted expert on the Millennial and college markets, she has written for *The Huffington Post, Seventeen* magazine, and *The Wall Street Journal,* and served as a philanthropy columnist for *USA Today.* Garton's brand and company have been featured in numerous media outlets, including the *Today* show. She has frequently been called upon to help select the nation's top 20 college students as a judge for *USA Today*'s All-USA College Academic Team, an award she received while in college, and has appeared as a guest speaker at numerous conferences, including a social entrepreneurship summit at the United Nations.